THE BEST WINES
IN THE
SUPER MARKETS
2025

NED HALLEY

foulsham
LONDON • NEW YORK • TORONTO • SYDNEY

W. Foulsham & Co. Ltd
for Foulsham Publishing Ltd
The Old Barrel Store, Drayman's Lane, Marlow, Bucks SL7 2FF

Foulsham books can be found in all good bookshops and direct from www.foulsham.com

ISBN: 978-0-572-04849-5

Printed and bound in Great Britain by Page Bros Ltd

Contents

Taking it seriously	5
It's all about the grape variety	9
Brand awareness	15
Wines of the year	17
Aldi	21
Asda	31
Co-op	37
Lidl	48
Majestic	53
Marks & Spencer	63
Morrisons	77
Sainsbury's	87
Tesco	96
Waitrose	114
Enjoying it	133
A wine vocabulary	138
Index	172

Taking it seriously

There's an old saying you don't hear so much these days that a meal without wine is like a day without sunshine. Oddly enough, it prevailed at a time when wine-drinking was an everyday pleasure in only a very few households, and wine was much more expensive than it is, in real terms, now. It was in the days, of course, before supermarkets got serious about selling wine.

I've been writing about this since the 1970s and can very well remember the big grocers waking up to the possibilities and taking on the established wine trade. Sainsbury's, whose London HQ was next door to the tower block of publishing giant IPC Magazines where I toiled, was the first to launch an own-label wine range and made jolly sure their news-thirsty neighbours got to hear about it.

Today, the supermarkets account for all but a fraction of the wine we drink at home. The grubby off-licences that once traded as extensions to pubs and even the biggest high-street chains like Peter Dominic and Victoria Wine are history.

It might have been a disaster for the quality and diversity of wines on offer for just a dozen or so giant retailers to control the market, but it's actually been a triumph. Throughout the 50 years since it all kicked off, the choice of wines in supermarkets has steadily widened, and the overall quality has just as consistently improved.

It is thanks to the market itself. From a country whose class system once dictated that wine was a commodity only for the wealthy, the educated or the widely travelled, Britain has calmly transformed into a wine-drinking nation. Yes of course it's because we're better-off, better educated (in some respects anyway) and definitely more widely travelled. But it's also down to the wine trade. It has kept up with the rising interest in wine and it has honoured that interest by providing variety and excellence. It has made this wonderful commodity everyday.

Affordability, naturally, remains the key, and the supermarkets know all about that. Fierce competition for customers makes it axiomatic that these retail giants buy everything to a price, and I am perpetually amazed that they manage to offer so many wines of such obvious quality at the prices they do.

Wine producers have a hard time dealing with supermarkets, in the UK as much as anywhere, but they can't do without them. Britain is among the biggest importers of wine in the world – regularly the number one, ahead even of the USA as well as all our continental neighbours – and the choice of wines in this country is easily the widest in any nation.

Tough though the business is, everyone seems to want a part of it. From the very beginning, landowners and aristocrats have hurried to get a few vines into their ground in pursuit of aesthetic ideals and exaltations. Farmers have sensibly followed suit, preferring the glory of the grape to the grind of agronomy. Multinational corporations have grown up around once-fragmented groups of small producers, especially in the 'New World'. And celebrities now take up the mantle: even in supermarkets you'll find wines made in the names of luminaries from Ian Botham to Kylie Minogue, Brad Pitt to Gordon Ramsay, Dolly Parton to Snoop Dogg.

The main point is that the supply side looks pretty secure. A very diverse collection of enterprises wishes to continue making wine, whatever the weather, whatever the temperance lobby says and however much governments (especially the British government) tries to tax alcohol out of existence.

In spite of the current difficulties, wine is looking pretty rosy. Tracking prices as I have been all these years – this annual edition of *The Best Wines in the Supermarkets* is the 21st – I can report that good wine is more available and no more expensive in real terms than it has ever been. It's true that UK excise duty has lately increased, but that was after a freeze of several years, and the way wine (and all other alcoholic drinks) is taxed has altered so that you pay more duty the higher the alcohol level in the product. But this is probably perfectly fair, and it doesn't seem to have impacted shelf prices all that dramatically.

In February 2025 the measures introduced by the previous government in August 2023 will be enacted in full, ending the transitional concession that all wines between 11.5% and 14.5% are taxed the same. Thereafter, the rates will be stepped. Whether retailers will increase the prices of higher-strength products remains to be seen, but what is already clear is that the number of wines of lower strength will certainly grow.

I have already tasted some of these, and there are a number recommended in the following pages. The wine trade is as alert as ever to changing circumstances, and I think we can all take comfort from it.

It's all about the grape variety

The grape, naturally, counts for everything in wine. The finished product is, after all, simply the fermented juice of the fruit. Well, yes, there will be a cultured yeast introduced to assist the process. And there are permitted additives, mostly sulphur products and clarifying agents, to ensure healthy, bright wine. The wine's natural sugars and acids can be supplemented.

But the grape variety still sets the pace. Dark-skinned grapes make red wine because the skins are included in the must (pressed juice) during fermentation and give the wine its colour. The juice of virtually all grapes is clear. You can make white wine with dark-skinned grapes by extracting the juice promptly and fermenting it free of the skins. The base wine for Champagne is made largely from dark-skinned grapes. But still white wine is made much more simply – from pale-skinned grapes fermented without their skins.

Different grape varieties produce correspondingly different wines. There are hundreds of distinct varieties, but a couple of dozen account for most production. All of us have favourites, or at least preferences. The varieties described here account for most of the wines on offer in the supermarkets.

Red wine varieties

Aglianico: Ancient variety of southern Italy said to have been imported by immigrant Greek farmers around 500 BC. The name is a recent rendering of former Ellenico ('Hellenic') and the grape has caught on again thanks to Aglianico del Vulture, a volcanic DOC of Basilicata. The wines are dark, intense, pungent and long-lived.

Barbera: The most widely planted dark-skinned grape of Piedmont in northwest Italy makes easy-drinking purple vigorous rasping red wine to enjoy young and also, increasingly, a darker, denser but still vigorous style given gravitas through oak-ageing. Mostly sold under denominations Barbera d'Asti and Barbera d'Alba. Unrelated to Barbaresco, a Piedmontese wine made from Nebbiolo grapes.

Cabernet Sauvignon: Originally of Bordeaux and the mainstay of claret, Cabernet berries are compact and thick-skinned, making wine of intense flavour and gripping tannin. The grandest wines need decades to develop their full bloom. Everyday wines made worldwide typically have dense colour, purple in youth, aromas of blackcurrants and cedar wood ('cigar box') and firm, juicy-savoury fruit.

Gamay: It's the grape of Beaujolais. Colour can be purple with a blue note; nose evokes new-squashed raspberries with perhaps a pear drop or two, the effect of carbonic maceration, the Beaujolais method of vinification. Fruit flavours are juicy, bouncing, even refreshing.

Grenache: The French name for the Garnacha, originally of Spain, where it is much employed in Rioja and other classic regions. HQ in France is the southern Rhône Valley with further widespread plantings across the country's Mediterranean regions. Wines can be light in colour but emphatic in flavour with a wild, hedgerow-fruit style lifted with spice and pepper. Widely cultivated across the New World.

Malbec: The signature grape of Argentina. A native of Bordeaux, where it plays a minor blending role, it thrives in the high-altitude vineyards of Mendoza, a province of the Andean foothills. The best wines have dark colour and a perfume sometimes fancifully said to evoke leather and liquorice; flavours embrace briary black fruits with suggestions of bitter chocolate, plum and spice.

Merlot: Bordeaux variety very often partnering Cabernet Sauvignon in claret blends and also solo in fabled Pomerol wines including Château Petrus. The grape is large and thin-skinned compared to Cabernet, making wine of rich ruby colour with scents evoking black cherry and cassis and fruit that can be round and rich. Ordinary wines are soft, mellow and early developing but might lack the firmness of tannin that gives balance.

Pinot Noir: It's the solo grape of proper red burgundy and one of three varieties in champagne. Everyday Pinot wines typically have a bright, translucent ruby colour and aromas evoking red soft summer fruits and cherries. Flavours correspond. Fine Pinot has elegant weight and shape, mysteriously alluring. New Zealand makes distinctive, delicious, sinewy Pinots; Chile produces robust and earthy Pinots; California's best Pinots compare for quality with fabulously expensive Burgundies.

Sangiovese: The grape of Chianti, so-named after the Latin for 'the blood of Jove', makes pleasingly weighted, attractively coloured wines with plummy perfume, even pruny in older wines, and slinky flavours evoking blackcurrant, raspberry and occasionally nectarine. Good Chianti always has a clear tannic edge, giving the wine its trademark nutskin-dry finish.

Syrah: At home in southern France, the Syrah makes wines that at their best are densely coloured, rich in aromas of sun-baked blackberries, silky in texture and plumply, darkly, spicily flavoured. The grandest pure-Syrah wines, such as Hermitage and Côte Rôtie, are gamey, ripe and rich and very long-lived. Syrah is widely planted across Mediterranean France as a blending grape in wines of the Côtes du Rhône and Languedoc. Under the name Shiraz, Syrah is Australia's most prolific red-wine variety.

Tempranillo: The grape at the heart of Rioja has to work hard. The unique selling point of the region's famous red wines is the long ageing process in oak casks that gives the finished product its creamy, vanilla richness – which can all too easily overwhelm the juiciness and freshness of the wine. The Tempranillo's bold blackcurranty-minty aromas and flavours stand up well to the test, and the grape's thick skin imparts handsome ruby colour that doesn't fade as well as firm tannins that keep the wine in shape even after many years in cask or bottle. Tempranillo is widely planted throughout Spain, and in Portugal, under numerous assumed names.

White wine varieties

Albariño: Rightly revered Iberian variety once better known in its Minho Valley, Portugal, manifestation as Alvarinho, a mainstay of vinho verde wine. Since the 1980s, Albariño from Spain's Galicia region, immediately north of Portugal, has been making aromatic and scintillatingly racy sea-fresh dry white wines from vineyards often planted close to the Atlantic shore. The seaside DO of Rias Baixas, now a major centre for gastro-tourism, is the heart of Albariño country. The variety, characterized by small, thick-skinned berries with many pips, is now also cultivated in California, New Zealand and beyond.

Chardonnay: Universal variety still at its best at home in Burgundy for simple appley fresh dry wines all the way up to lavish new-oak-fermented deluxe appellations such as Meursault and Montrachet making ripe, complex, creamy-nutty and long-developing styles. Imitated in Australia and elsewhere with mixed success.

Chenin Blanc: Loire Valley variety cultivated for dry, sweet and sparkling white wines, some of them among France's finest. Honeyed aromas and zesty acidity equally characterize wines including elegant, mineral AOP Vouvray and opulent, golden late-harvested AOP Coteaux du Layon. In South Africa, Chenin Blanc now makes many fascinating and affordable wines.

Fiano: Revived southern Italian variety makes dry but nuanced wines of good colour with aromas of orchard fruit, almonds and candied apricots and finely balanced fresh flavours. Fleetingly fashionable and worth seeking out.

Glera: Widely planted in the Veneto region of northeast Italy, it's the principal variety in prosecco sparkling wine. The grape itself used to be named prosecco, after the winemaking village of Prosecco near Treviso, but under a 2009 change to the wine-denomination rules, the name can now be applied exclusively to the wine, not the grape. Glera makes a neutral base wine with plenty of acidity. It is a prolific variety, and needs to be. Sales of prosecco in Britain have now surpassed those of champagne.

Palomino Fino: The grape that makes sherry. The vines prosper in the *albariza*, the sandy, sun-bleached soil of Andalucia's Jerez region, providing a pale, bone-dry base wine ideally suited to the sherry process. All proper sherry of every hue is white wine from Palomino Fino. The region's other grape, the Pedro Ximenez, is used as a sweetening agent and to make esoteric sweet wines.

Pinot Grigio: At home in northeast Italy, it makes dry white wines of pale colour and frequently pale flavour too. The mass-market wines' popularity might owe much to their natural low acidity. The better wines are aromatic, fleetingly smoky and satisfyingly weighty in the manner of Pinot Gris made in the French province of Alsace. New Zealand Pinot Gris or Pinot Grigio follows the Alsace style.

Riesling: Native to Germany, it makes unique wines pale in colour with sharp-apple aromas and racy, sleek fruit whether dry or sweet according to labyrinthine local winemaking protocols. Top-quality Rhine and Mosel Rieslings age wonderfully, taking on golden hues and a fascinating 'petrolly' resonance. Antipodean Rieslings have more colour and weight often with a mineral, limey twang.

Sauvignon Blanc: Currently fashionable thanks to New Zealand's inspired adoption of the variety for assertive, peapod-nettle-seagrass styles. Indigenous Sauvignons from France's Loire Valley have rapidly caught up, making searingly fresh wines at all levels from generic Touraine up to high-fallutin' Sancerre. Delicate, elegant Bordeaux Sauvignon is currently on top form too.

Semillon: Along with Sauvignon Blanc, a key component of white Bordeaux, including late-harvested, golden sweet wines such as Sauternes. Even in dry wines, colour ranges up to rich yellow, aromas evoke tropical fruits and honeysuckle, exotic flavours lifted by citrus presence. Top Australian Semillons rank among the world's best.

Viognier: Formerly fashionable but perpetually interesting variety of the Rhône Valley makes white wines of pleasing colour with typical apricot aroma and almondy-orchardy fruit; styles from quite dry to fruitily plump.

More about these varieties and many others in 'A wine vocabulary' starting on page 138.

Brand awareness

Big-brand wines such as Blossom Hill and Hardy do not crowd the pages of this book. I do get to taste them, and leave most of them out. I believe they don't measure up for quality, interest or value.

The best wines in the supermarkets are very often own-brands. Own-brands date back to the 1970s, when interest in wine finally began to take root in Britain. Sainsbury's was first, with its own Claret, about 1975. It was hardly a revolutionary idea. Grand merchants like Berry Bros & Rudd (est 1698) had been doing own-label Bordeaux and much else besides, for ever.

In the supermarket sector, wine was bought on the wholesale market like anything else, from butter to washing powder. Only when interest in wine started to extend beyond the coterie served by the merchants did the mass retailers take any notice. It was thanks, of course, to the new craze for foreign travel, and to the good influence of writers like Elizabeth David, who revealed the joys of Continental-style food and drink. In 1966, Hugh Johnson's brilliant and accessible book *Wine* piqued the public consciousness as never before.

The adoption of supermarket wine was slow enough, but accelerated in the 1980s by the arrival of new, decent wines from Australia. Earlier on, cheap Aussie wines had been overripe, stewed rubbish, but breakthrough technology now enabled fresh, bold reds and whites of a different stripe. Wretched Europlonk brands like Hirondelle retreated before a tide of lush Chardonnay and 'upfront' Shiraz.

The horizon for supermarket wine buyers, always shackled by price constraint, was suddenly widened. In spite of the delivery distances, southern hemisphere producers could match their Old World counterparts for value as well as interest and quality.

In time, the winemakers of Europe fought back. Top estates carried on with 'fine wine' production, but humbler enterprises had to learn how to master real quality at the everyday level. They did. I believe the huge improvements in the simpler wines of the Continent owe much to the need to match the competition from the New World.

By the 1990s, Britain had become the world's biggest wine importer. Supermarkets were largely responsible, and now had muscle in the market. They started to dispatch their own people to vineyards and wineries worldwide, not just to buy the wines but to participate in their production. And always, they demanded the lowest-possible prices.

And so to today's proliferation of supermarket own-brands. They are the flagships of every one of the big grocers, and usually the focal point of promotions. They are, naturally enough, the wines of which their begetters are most proud. Mass-market brands do still persist in the supermarkets. Some are very good. I think of Blason, Chasse and Vieille Ferme from France; Baron de Ley and Miguel Torres from Spain; McGuigan and Penfolds from Australia; Catena from Argentina and Concha y Toro from Chile, among others.

If you have a favourite popular brand, do check the index to this book on page 172. It might not be mentioned in the entry for the supermarket where you're used to finding it, but that doesn't mean I've left it out.

Wines of the year

Thirty-four top scores this year are distributed with the customary randomness between nations and retailers. The key, please remember, is value for money. If the gongs were bestowed according to the wines I'd liked best regardless of price, a lot of the names here would be absent. This is my Top 34 for wine lovers on a budget.

The order for origin is France first with 11 maximum scores, Italy a close runner-up with 10 then Portugal and Spain with 3 apiece and Australia with 2. Argentina, Chile, England and Germany each win 1.

Retailer ranks are revealing. Tesco and Waitrose tie on 9 apiece. This is the first time in 21 editions of this guide that Waitrose has not had pole position to itself. A sign of the times? Certainly, credit is due to Tesco. Runners-up are Co-op, M&S and Morrisons each on 3, Aldi and Asda both on 2 and singletons for Lidl, Majestic and Sainsbury's.

Another first this year is the inaugural top score for a rosé. It goes to M&S's La Dame en Rose Rosé 2023 at £7.00. A Languedoc wine from carignan grapes, it stood out from more than a hundred rosés I've tasted over the summer of 2024 as genuinely delicious and fairly priced. I dare say it proves that seven quid is as much as you need to spend on a bottle of pink wine. But maybe I shouldn't. The infatuation for rosé is a boon to winemakers and they're entitled to exploit it.

Red wines

Lateral Pinot Noir	Tesco	£4.39
Villa Verde Montepulciano d'Abruzzo 2022	Morrisons	£6.00
M&S Montepulciano d'Abruzzo 2020	M&S	£6.50
Heredad del Rey Monastrell Syrah 2020	Waitrose	£6.99
Co-op Fairtrade Cabernet Sauvignon 2023	Co-op	£7.50
Specially Selected Coteaux de Béziers Merlot Syrah 2023	Aldi	£8.49
Vino Nobile di Montepulciano 2020	Lidl	£8.99
The Best Chinon 2023	Morrisons	£9.00
Palladino Molise Biferno Riserva 2019	Co-op	£9.50
Terre de Fiano Organic Primitivo 2022	Waitrose	£10.99
Wirra Wirra Church Block 2020	Asda	£11.50
Pazzia Primitivo del Manduria 2021	Waitrose	£12.99
Château St Hilaire Médoc 2019	Waitrose	£15.99
Finest Margaux 2019	Tesco	£24.00

Pink wine

M&S La Dame en Rose Rosé 2023	M&S	£7.50

White wines

Dr L Riesling 2022	Asda	£6.50
Blueprint Vinho Verde 2023	Waitrose	£6.99
Duffour Père et Fils Vinum Côtes de Gascogne 2023	Majestic	£6.99
M&S Found Lucido 2023	M&S	£7.50
Finest Stellenbosch Chenin Blanc 2023	Tesco	£8.00
Finest Soave Classico Superiore 2022	Tesco	£8.25
Taste the Difference Sicilia Grillo 2023	Sainsbury's	£8.75
St Mont Grande Cuvée 2020	Tesco	£9.50
La Perrière Touraine Sauvignon Blanc 2023	Waitrose	£9.99
Tre Fiori Greco di Tufo 2022	Waitrose	£11.99
Tyrell's Brookdale Hunter Valley Semillon 2022	Tesco	£15.00

Fortified wines

The Best Palo Cortado Sherry 37.5cl	Morrisons	£7.25
Finest Ten-Year-Old Tawny Port	Tesco	£14.50
Graham's Ten-Year-Old Tawny Port	Waitrose	£23.49

Sparkling wines

Contevedo Cava Brut	Aldi	£5.45
Gratien & Meyer Crémant d'Alsace Brut	Tesco	£12.50
Les Pionniers Champagne Brut	Co-op	£21.50
Chapel Down Brut NV	Waitrose	£28.99
Finest Vintage Grand Cru Champagne Brut 2017	Tesco	£30.00

Aldi

Aldi means business. The first UK store opened as recently as 1990, but the network already has more than a thousand outlets and sales lately overtook those of Morrisons. Aldi is now our fourth largest supermarket chain.

The wines used to be borderline and didn't make it into the pages of this guide until the 2015 edition. But there have been improvements. It's still a comparatively narrow range, under 200, but every wine is exclusive and it's getting more various including a new 'Unearthed' selection from off-the-beaten-track sources.

In the round, I can't say Aldi wines are really any cheaper than other supermarkets' offerings. As 'entry level' fixed costs and excise duty make up so much of retail price, wines around the £5 mark are no more plentiful at Aldi than anywhere else. But upscale a bit this retailer certainly competes in value as well as quality and interest.

My favourites this year are mainly from the mid-price bracket, starting with a Midi red Specially Selected Coteaux de Béziers Syrah Merlot 2023 at £8.49, marvellously made for the money and giving the lie to the persisting falsehood that merlot is passé. At the same price I strongly commend Italian red Specially Selected Castel del Monte Rosso 2022 from nero di troia, a grape variety that prospers in Puglia and deserves to be better known.

At a modest £5.99 one of my top whites is Baron Amarillo Rueda Verdejo 2023, a genuinely delicious aromatic dry wine from northwest Spain's rightly renowned Rueda region. The Baron Amarillo brand, long extended across Aldi's Spanish range, could surely do with an update, but this is a cracking wine that anyone seeking a sensibly priced alternative to sauvignon should try.

In the bargain basement, Aldi does my budget fizz of the year, Contevedo Cava Brut at just £5.45. It comes in a rather odd, silvered bottle, but makes prosecco look flat and is as lively and interesting as countless sparklers of far greater pretension.

You might not find every wine recommended here in every store, but Aldi has an accessible website (by which I mean one on which a computer no-hoper like me can successfully order wine online for home delivery) offering the whole range.

RED WINES

8 Specially Selected Buenas Vides Organic Argentinan Malbec 2023 £7.99

Proper chewy rounded black-fruit winter wine of savoury darkness in what is now the well-established Mendoza style; 13.5% alcohol.

8 Kooliburra Australian Shiraz Cabernet 2022 £4.89

Unexpectedly healthy and harmonious everyday blend with generous ripe black fruits and just 11% alcohol at a very keen price.

8 Chapter & Verse Merlot 2022 £5.25

You get the trademark black-cherry sweetness of the merlot but it's lively and bright on the palate, an artful Aussie party red at such a good price; 11% alcohol.

8 Specially Selected Coonawarra Cabernet Sauvignon 2022 £7.99

Massively ripe, blackcurranty, pure cabernet; nicely poised, not at all cooked, and juicily delicious in a muscular sort of way; 14.5% alcohol.

8 Specially Selected Australian Cabernet Franc 2022 £8.99

The cabernet franc grape of Loire Valley and Bordeaux fame must be a bit of an outsider in Australia. The label on this one helps with the phonetic pronunciation 'cab-err-nay-fronk'. It's a good translation: supple black berry fruit with the grape's trademark stalkiness, sleek and a versatile food match; 14% alcohol.

RED WINES

♉ 9 Estevez Chilean Merlot 2022 £4.29

At this price I didn't hold out much hope, but here's a merlot with plenty of mouthfilling berry fruit defined by gentle tannin, and lasting in savour; 13% alcohol. Top value.

♉ 8 Estevez Chilean Malbec 2022 £5.79

This darkly juicy blend with syrah has decent weight and grip: an attractive plump-fruit Chilean variation on the tougher Argentine malbec style; 12.5% alcohol.

♉ 8 Estevez Chilean Pinot Noir 2023 £6.99

Chilean pinot can artfully combine New World ripeness with poise and lightness; this one, from the Casablanca Valley, fits the bill: juicy raspberry fruit trim at the edge; 14% alcohol.

CHILE

♉ 8 Pierre Jaurant Bordeaux 2021 £5.29

Mature-tasting generic claret of wholesome blackcurrant savour with depth and grip; 13% alcohol. Rare find at this sort of price.

♉ 10 Specially Selected Coteaux de Béziers Merlot Syrah 2023 £8.49

A Mediterranean merlot with one-third slinky syrah that works wonders: deep purple young wine with black-cherry and hedgerow-fruit richness trimmed by firm but friendly tannin; tastes long and classy; 14% alcohol. Seek this one out for meaty menus, as recommended by my good friend Olly Smith as the perfect partner for my son Max's Mega Meatloaf Sandwich on that excellent BBC culinary show _Saturday Kitchen_.

♉ 8 Specially Selected Ventoux Rouge 2022 £8.49

Ventoux is an appellation of the Rhône making dependably warm and spicy reds; this is a good example at a fair price; 14.5% alcohol.

FRANCE

RED WINES

Y 8 Castellore Primitivo 2022   £6.29
Sweetly ripe plummy Puglian with a good grip; 13.5% alcohol.
Better buy than Aldi's Primitivo di Manduria at £9.99.

Y 8 Specially Selected Toscana Rosso 2022   £7.99
The labelling rather resembles that of Tignanello, the original
'super Tuscan' of the 1970s devised by Chianti aristos Antinori,
and the blend's the same too – local sangiovese with cabernet
and merlot – and it's all good fun at a fraction of the price;
14% alcohol.

Y 9 Specially Selected Castel del Monte Rosso 2022   £8.49
Classy Puglian from the DOC of Castel del Monte, the region's
premier zone for reds from the nero di Troia grape, renowned
(but underreported) for its plum and violet aromas, succulent
dark fruit and friendly tannins; this is a good one with a
choccy-liquorice note, creamy, sleek and long; 13.5% alcohol.
The name nero di Troia (black of Troy) probably originates
from the Puglian town of Troia, supposedly founded by ancient
Greeks back from conquering Troy in the 13th century BCE.
Note however that the modern Italian word *troia* means
'harlot'.

Y 8 Animus Douro 2021   £6.49
This table wine from Port country does echo the darkly sweet
and spicy style of the fortified version with a light touch; 13%
alcohol.

Y 8 Mimo Moutinho Dão 2021   £6.69
Proper Portuguese table red from the remote Dão region owing
its dark porty aromas and heft to constituent grapes touriga
nacional and tinta roriz, piqued with mint and gentle spices, all
with a relishable tension; 13% alcohol.

ITALY

PORTUGAL

RED WINES

SOUTH AFRICA

🍷 8 **Cambalala Fairhand Shiraz Pinotage 2022**   £6.29
Curry-night red with a good lick of tarry pinotage (the Cape's own black grape) amid the dark blackberry savours; 13.5% alcohol.

SPAIN

🍷 8 **Baron Amarillo Rioja Reserva 2018**   £6.29
Pleasantly slick mature savours in which the cassis fruit holds up well with the vanilla oak; artful, cheap and 13.5% alcohol.

🍷 9 **Unearthed Cigales Crianza 2020**   £9.99
Aldi is following M&S's 'Found' range with its own 'Unearthed' wines from less-known places with this fine tinta del pais (tempranillo) from Cigales, neglected neighbour to chi-chi Ribera del Duero region. It's big, earthy and brimming with blackcurrant ripeness, sleek with oak contact and nicely tannin trimmed; 14% alcohol.

PINK WINES

FRANCE

🍷 8 **Specially Selected Coteaux de Béziers Rosé 2023**   £8.49
My pick out of half a dozen rather similar Mediterranean rosés tasted at Aldi is from cinsault and grenache grapes giving good bold colour, rose-petal and strawberry whiffs and fresh red fruit with a bit of crunch as well as sunny warmth; 12.5% alcohol.

ITALY

🍷 8 **Specially Selected Costa Toscana Rosé 2023**   £7.99
It's pink Chianti, in effect, made mainly from the black sangiovese grape of Tuscany's famed flask wine, and it does have some of the cherry-raspberry juiciness of the red while still managing to taste fresh and bright and, yes, pink; 12.5% alcohol.

WHITE WINES

8 **Chapter & Verse Chardonnay 2022** £5.25
It comes in a flat flask format from recyclable plastic but there's no gimmick to the healthy and plump sweet-apple fruit balanced by citrus lift; just 11% alcohol and seriously cheap.

9 **Specially Selected Austrian Grüner Veltliner 2023** £8.19
Impressive smoky style to this exotic just-dry herbaceous and orchard-fruity aperitif wine (also a natural with spicy dishes) from GV, Austria's distinctive indigenous white grape variety; 12.5% alcohol. One of a great pair of new Aldi wines from Austria's prime Niederosterreich region.

9 **Specially Selected Austrian Riesling 2022** £8.49
Plushly ripe and yet racy crisp-fruit classic Riesling of delicious texture and balance; 12.5% alcohol. Fine aperitif and equally a food-matcher – great match for roast chicken.

8 **Specially Selected Chilean Chardonnay 2023** £6.99
Wholesome Casablanca wine with the Chilean signature ripeness embellished by 'toasted oak' contact – seductive in style and price; 14% alcohol.

8 **Specially Selected English White Cuvée 2022** £9.99
Crikey, this isn't bad, says my note on this expensive but ripe and distinctive blend of unfamiliar grapes from Devon: it's a picnic of fresh orchard-fruit flavours, dry but not green, tangy but not sharp; easy to like and just 11.5% alcohol.

8 **Specially Selected Coteaux de Béziers
Viognier Grenache** £8.49
Softly lush but well-balanced Mediterranean blend; warm apricot-peach fruit lifted by artful citrus twang; 13% alcohol.

WHITE WINES

FRANCE

♟ 8 **Specially Selected Le Bourgeron Chardonnay 2023**   £8.49
Safe bet Pays d'Oc has plumpness of sweet-apple and peach fruit with vivid freshness besides; 13.5% alcohol.

♟ 8 **Specially Selected Picpoul de Pinet 2023**   £8.49
Particularly lively and crisp rendering of this fashionable Mediterranean slaker; good salinity and zing; 12.5% alcohol.

♟ 8 **Specially Selected Luberon Blanc 2023**   £8.99
Lushly textured nectarine-pineapple-peach dry wine in the likeable white-Rhône style; a versatile food matcher and full of sunny interest; 13% alcohol.

GREECE

♟ 8 **Athlon Assyrtiko 2023**   £8.99
Aldi don't miss a trick: a dry, pleasingly abrasive refresher from Macedonia plumped up with a portion of chardonnay to enhance the savour of the trendy assyrtiko (Greece's flagship white grape); 12% alcohol.

ITALY

♟ 8 **Unearthed Bianco di Custoza 2023**   £9.99
From the new off-the-beaten-track range, an emphatically juicy dry wine from Lake Garda made largely from Soave grape garganega and echoing the apple-lemon-blanched-almond of the famed Verona wine; 12% alcohol. I liked it, even at the ambitious price.

NEW ZEALAND

♟ 8 **Specially Selected Marlborough Sauvignon Blanc 2022**   £7.69
Brisk peapod and seagrass style, every bit as interesting as big-name brands; 12.5% alcohol.

WHITE WINES

SOUTH AFRICA

8 | **Cambala South African Sauvignon Blanc 2023**   £5.49
Crisp and bright with sunny gooseberry fruit. Scores for grassy-crunchy, green, tangy but satisfyingly ripened, proper sauvignon style; 12.5% alcohol.

8 | **Grapevine Chardonnay**   £4.09
I approached this non-vintage 'entry-level' dry white with caution but it's entirely legit, even recognisable as chardonnay (not a variety much expected from Spain) from the soft-apple nose and fresh peachy fruit; just 11% alcohol and as cheerful as it is cheap.

SPAIN

9 | **Baron Amarillo Rueda Verdejo 2023**   £5.99
Attractively coloured (*amarillo* is Spanish for 'yellow'), dry, saline, green-fruit refresher from rightly prestigious Rueda region – natural home to the verdejo vine, Spain's convincing answer to everyone else's ubiquitous sauvignon; 13% alcohol.

SPARKLING WINES

FRANCE

9 | **Specially Selected Crémant de Jura Brut 2020**   £8.99
Aldi likes to mention a recent report favouring this excellent pure chardonnay sparkler from the Jura mountains east of Burgundy over Laurent-Perrier champagne costing £40 more. It's certainly a smart package: creamy mousse, full ripe red-apple fruit with yeasty trace, balanced and elegant; 12% alcohol.

SPARKLING WINES

FRANCE

🍷 8 **Specially Selected Crémant de Bordeaux Rosé** **£8.99**
You don't see much sparkling Bordeaux these days but here's a pink 'un worth discovering: properly made from merlot and cabernet franc grapes, it's busily 'creaming' in its sparkle, delicately coloured with an elusive strawberry perfume and ripe but crisp, dry and refreshing; 12% alcohol.

🍷 8 **Veuve Monsigny Champagne Brut** **£14.99**
Wildly fizzy and saucily sweet (in a good way) a consistently appealing, balanced proper non-vintage house champagne at an appealing price; 12.5% alcohol.

ITALY

🍷 7 **Castellone Organic Prosecco** **£7.19**
If you like the prosecco style try this soft sparkler for its peary freshness and, even more so, for its sensible price; 11.5% alcohol.

🍷 8 **Fiori di Rosa** **£8.99**
Not all Italian fizz is Prosecco. Try this alternative rosé from the same region, Veneto, but from a blend of garganega grapes (source of Soave) and merlot (big player in claret): pale blossom pink colour, busy fizz, crisp entry and plump-pear fruit; fun fizz at a fair price; 11% alcohol.

SPAIN

🍷 10 **Contevedo Cava Brut** **£5.45**
It comes in a strange silvered bottle but this quality cava, made by the same method as champagne, has attractive full colour, persistent mousse and a delicious flush of stone-fruit and citrus savour; 11.5% alcohol. The price is astounding: cheaper now than it was three years ago when I featured it to an enthusiastic audience on Channel 4's *Sunday Brunch* show. The best bargain fizz on the market.

Asda

Asda is in the news. The sale in 2021 by previous American owner Walmart of 90 per cent of the shares to petrol-forecourt moguls the Issa brothers has not coincided with any uplift in the Leeds-based retail giant's fortunes. One of the two Issas, Zuber, sold his stake in 2024 to their private-equity backer TDR, leaving the other, Mohsin, with less than a quarter of the equity and control of the business in the hands of, well, a firm of London financiers.

Who cares? Certainly Asda's vast number of employees and suppliers do. And Asda has always inspired loyalty among its customers, first in the north when the company was launched by Yorkshire farmers and butchers in the 1960s, and soon farther and farther afield as it expanded nationwide to become one of the Big Four grocers.

There were ups and downs and the takeover by the world's biggest grocer Walmart in 1999, but Asda was a serious contender in every respect. In the 2015 edition of this guide, I wrote: 'As far as wine goes, Asda is on equal terms, at the very least, with its rivals among the Big Four supermarkets'.

I cannot report on Asda's wine offering with the same enthusiasm today, especially as I am no longer invited to the company's press tastings. But I have visited three Asda stores, inspected the wines, pounced when price reductions have made the reluctant outlay less painful, and assembled the following recommendations in a spirit of optimism and fairplay.

RED WINES

ARGENTINA

🍷 8   **Malbado Malbec 2022**   **£15.50**

This extravagant oaked Mendoza varietal feels fully developed in spite of its relative youth, with lusciously rounded intense malbec savours evoking bitter chocolate, new leather, the lot, and yet tightly defined and balanced; 14% alcohol. Pricy but I got mine for £12.50 on promo.

AUSTRALIA

🍷 8   **Extra Special Barossa Shiraz 2022**   **£9.00**

Full-bodied but trimly balanced, cushiony-ripe and wholesome spicy-rich true-to-Barossa-style wine for meaty occasions; 14.5% alcohol.

🍷 10   **Wirra Wirra Church Block 2020**   **£11.50**

No hesitation in reprising this renowned Cabernet-Shiraz-Merlot from the McLaren Vale – and the price is down 10 per cent from last year's £13. Thrilling blackcurrant/blackberry cushiony and spiced fruit with notions of pungent olive and cigar-box; 14.5% alcohol. It's amazing value.

CHILE

🍷 8   **Cono Sur Bicicleta Pinot Noir 2022**   **£7.00**

Big-brand but eco (winery workers all on bikes) bargain; juicy and earthy in the best pinot tradition; light in colour, weight and woof (just 11% alcohol) but full of ripe summer red fruits.

🍷 8   **Extra Special Leyda Valley Pinot Noir 2022**   **£9.25**

Soft and plump but with a firm backbone, an impressively complex variation on the cherry-raspberry pinot theme with a nice tight finish to make it an ideal match for rich poultry dishes; 13.5% alcohol.

RED WINES

8 Extra Special Beaujolais Cru Fleurie 2022   £11.00
Jolly juicy-purply Beaujolais made under the chi-chi AP of
Fleurie that looks cheap at the price (I paid £10 on promo) but
in fairness this is more the kind of wine you'd expect under the
humbler Beaujolais-Villages AP. Likeable just the same, silky
and long; 13.5% alcohol.

8 La Mora Maremma Toscana Rosso 2020   £10.00
Maremma is the coastal neighbour of the Chianti zone of
Tuscany and makes interesting red wines from the Chianti
grape, sangiovese, often blended with Bordeaux varieties as
this one is. Pleasing smooth blackcurrant-sour-cherry-plum
fruits; 14% alcohol.

8 Nice Drop Shiraz 2022   £4.25
The prices for Asda's entry-level Nice Drop range are
incomprehensible at £4.25 across the board but this wine is
easy to like. It's a surprise to find it hails from Spain, as shiraz
is really an exclusively Australian synonym for Europe's syrah
grape. Perky, brambly, party red in balance with modest 11%
alcohol.

**8 Extra Special Marques del Norte Rioja
Reserva 2019   £9.00**
Made by Bodega El Coto, who also do the Riojas for M&S, it's
sleek, smoky and minty cassis-rich in the approved manner with
the vanilla oakiness nicely in the background; 14% alcohol.

PINK WINES

8 Wine Atlas Ile de Beauté Rosé 2023   £7.00
Delicate shell-pink colour and zippy freshness in this good-
value Corsican wine; floral notes, white peach and citrussy lift;
11% alcohol.

33

PINK WINES

9 La Vieille Ferme Rosé 2023 £8.50

From one of the most widely distributed – and widely admired – French brands, the new vintage of this delightful Rhône pink is as fresh as ever but with plenty of fruit interest – strawberry and redcurrant teamed with crisp white savours and tingly citrus – and brisk at the finish; 13% alcohol. Frequently on promo at Asda and elsewhere.

8 Viña Albali Tempranillo Rosado 2023 £5.50

Shameless magenta colour, jolly whiff of strawberry and a juicy summer-red fruitiness that will compete well with most al fresco feasts, this La Mancha pink is generous rather than sweet in style and trimmed with an artful acidity; 11.5% alcohol. As good as rosé gets at this price level.

WHITE WINES

8 Extra Special Chardonnay 2022 £8.75

Dependable Barossa Valley pure chardonnay, reportedly part-fermented in barriques. It has a certain white-nut oak creaminess gilding the bright apple/peach fruit; 13.5% alcohol.

8 Cono Sur Bicicleta Viognier 2023 £7.00

Nicely weighted in spite of the lower-alcohol (11%) of this likeable range; a rather lush apricot-peach dry style with trim acidity to finish. Widely available, but Asda's price is the fairest.

8 Paul Mas Marsanne Pays d'Oc 2023 £8.75

This hefty Mediterranean varietal from lush white Rhône grape marsanne intensifies exotic-stone-fruit with blanched-nut creaminess lifted by citrus acidity; artful as you'd expect from ingenious Paul Mas and a heady match for salads and rich dishes as well fish and fowl; 13% alcohol. I paid £7.50 on promo.

WHITE WINES

FRANCE

🍷 **9** **Extra Special Touraine Sauvignon Blanc 2022** **£9.00**
Touraine is the generic AP for Loire wines including plenty of genuinely delicious sauvignons, some easily comparable to famous regional names such as Sancerre. Try this one: crisply zesty even on the nose with classic crunchy green-pepper and gooseberry lushness carried along by pebbly river freshness; 13% alcohol. Not cheap but I paid £7.75 on routine promo.

🍷 **9** **Trimbach Riesling 2020** **£17.50**
My spies have found the 2019 as well as this 2020 on shelf and either will serve well. The 2020 is richly coloured and correspondingly intense in its apple-pear fruit of proper Alsace pungency and raciness ornamented by suggestions of tropical fruit, wood smoke and citrus acidity; remarkable stuff that will live long and evolve, 13% alcohol.

GERMANY

🍷 **10** **Dr L Riesling 2022** **£6.50**
Top marks to Asda for persisting with this yardstick Mosel, full of red-apple zing and prickly freshness in this new vintage from world-class winemaker Dr Ernie Loosen. And well done Asda, too, for passing on the benefit of 2023's reduction of excise duty on lower-alcohol wines; this 8.5% alcohol wine is 50p cheaper than it was last year. And that truly is a bargain.

NEW ZEALAND

🍷 **9** **Kakapo White 2023** **£6.25**
Named in honour of New Zealand's galumphing, flightless and critically endangered native green parrot (depicted on the label) this riesling-based blend with chardonnay and semillon cleverly unites exotic fruit with raciness and zest; an unexpected pleasure at a keen price; 12% alcohol.

🍷 **8** **Yealands Sauvignon Blanc 2023** **£9.75**
Marlborough producer Yealands can be counted on. Bright and zesty pure varietal bringing nettly zing to ripe green fruit with peachy notes and lingering grassy lushness; 12.5% alcohol.

WHITE WINES

ROMANIA

🍷 8 **Wine Atlas Feteasca Regala** £6.00

The last survivor from Asda's original inspired Wine Atlas range from off-beat sources, launched a decade ago, progressively neglected and in 2024, suddenly relaunched with a handful of new introductions and more, reportedly, to come. This one's a bargain tropical-fruit off-dry wine with balancing freshness and tang from Romania's flagship white grape; 11.5% alcohol.

SPAIN

🍷 8 **Palacio de Vivero Verdejo Rueda 2023** £6.75

Long, leesy and lemony rendering of the rightly revered Rueda dry white from verdejo grapes; first-choice summer-holiday wine for fish and trickier menus including salads and cured meats; 13% alcohol.

SPARKLING WINES

FRANCE

🍷 8 **Veuve Olivier & Fils Secret de Cave**
Champagne Brut £28.00

The secret is out: Asda's non-vintage champagne is really good: vigorous mousse and vigorous fruit too, teaming crisp orchard fruits with bright citrus highlights and a friendly yeasty theme to aroma and savour; 12.5% alcohol.

SPAIN

🍷 8 **Asda Cava Brut** £7.00

Floral nose with a little bakery warmth leading into fully fizzing crisp orchard-fruit savours with mellow peachy notes and a twangy citrus lift; nicely made and easy to like; 12% alcohol.

Co-op

It's Co-op this year at the top of this page. Last year it was The Co-op, and all the years before, The Co-operative. It can't be abbreviated any further, surely. If the corporate-image brigade try to take the hyphen out, I'll refuse to co-operate.

Only joshing. Co-op is wonderful. The wine range is doing the very opposite of abbreviating and the way the wines are merchandised in stores – more than 2,000 of them – is being impressively updated. Online wine retailing has yet to take off – a pity when so many of the best wines are available in only a fraction of the total number of outlets – but a new feature in 2024 is the introduction of online member wine tastings. Look online, obvs, for details.

It's a pleasure to be commending several Fairtrade wines here this year, particularly in what is the 20th anniversary of the first Co-op listing of a Fairtrade wine. Did you know Co-op is the world's largest seller of Fairtrade wine? Appropriately enough one of my top scores this year goes to Co-op Fairtrade Cabernet Sauvignon 2023 from Argentina at £7.50 and I very much like a new fizz from the same producer, Co-op Fairtrade Tilimuqui Sparkling Brut at £9.50.

Other highlights include the new 2022 vintage of Co-op Irresistible Chablis, made by Jean-Marc Brocard, whom followers of this great Burgundy appellation will know for his exceptional output, is particularly special and, believe it or not, rather good value at £15.50.

Back on earth, I strongly commend Co-op Irresistble Carignan 2022 from Chile at £8.00. Carignan is a widely planted but rarely identified blending grape of the south of France, and in South America it's being given a well-deserved day in the sunshine. This is a special wine.

RED WINES

🍷 **10** **Co-op Fairtrade Cabernet Sauvignon 2023** £7.50
From the La Riojana co-operative in the Famatina Valley, lost in the foothills of the Andes, a superb bargain: blood-red colour; opulent, ripe but ideally poised blackcurrant fruit, including a proportion brought up in new oak casks, and a definition of balance that's an object lesson; 13% alcohol. Fairtrade wine more than fairly priced.

🍷 **9** **Co-op Fairtrade Irresistible Organic**
Malbec 2021 £8.50
Very dark purple and generous briar, bitter-chocolate, blackberry-pie (rich pastry included) construct by La Riojana. A worthy successor to last year's 2020 vintage, and already mellowing nicely with a bit of bottle age; such a likeable wine; 13% alcohol.

🍷 **8** **Tilimuqui Malbec 2023** £8.50
La Riojana again with this beetroot-red, sweetly ripe blend of malbec with one-tenth bonarda, a healthy, brisk-finishing Fairtrade wine of convincing quality; 13% alcohol.

ARGENTINA

🍷 **8** **Co-op Lime Tree Australian Shiraz 2023** £6.00
Cheap-looking party red maybe, but it's a jolly vigorous and darkly juicy glassful for the money; 13% alcohol.

🍷 **8** **Andrew Peace Shiraz 2023** £7.00
Oaked shiraz-tempranillo blend: plumply ripe but nicely defined in its bramble-blackcurrant fruit and rather elegantly weighted; 13.5% alcohol.

🍷 **9** **Interlude Pinot Noir 2023** £8.65
Purity of fruit is the theme here, a beguiling raspberry-cherry plumpness twanged with pinot edginess and instantly recognisable', I write, and then see in the note it has 13% shiraz added to it. A real charmer just the same, though, and just 11% alcohol.

AUSTRALIA

RED WINES

8   **Bethany 6 Gen Old Vine Grenache 2023**   £12.50
The colour's just north of rosé but this is very proper berry-cherry intense grippy full-bodied satisfying red wine from the Barossa, and full of pleasant surprises; 14.5% alcohol. Unusually, an Aussie red that will respond well to chilling for warmer occasions.

9   **Co-op Irresistible Carignan 2022**   £8.00
Vanilla from oak contact intrudes immediately on the nose but it works very well in tandem with the blueberry/fruits-of-the-forest piquancy amid the robust cassis savour of this interesting and thoroughly individual Maule Valley food red; 14% alcohol. Scores for value and for varietal diversity.

8   **Co-op Irresistible Carménère 2022**   £8.00
Darkly sumptuous in colour and texture as is to be hoped from a Chilean carmenère (French for 'carmine'), a new Co-op line at a good price. Warm spicy black fruits with a friendly grip; 14% alcohol.

8   **Co-op Côtes du Rhône 2022**   £6.65
Pale but firmly weighted warmly spicy and ripe briar-black-fruit wine unpretentiously presented but convincingly intense; 13.5% alcohol.

9   **Domaine des Ormes Saumur 2022**   £10.50
This elusive Loire red is worth seeking out – look online for your nearest Co-op stockist – for its vivid blueberry-perfumed purply juicy but substantially intense fruit marked by a delicious stalky-leafy freshness of savour; 12.5% alcohol.

RED WINES

FRANCE

🍷 8 Château Chapelle d'Aliénor 2019 £14.50
If I've got this right, this wine is made at a very grand St Emilion estate, Château Gaffelière, as a declassified sideline under the humble appellation of Bordeaux Supérieur. Mostly merlot, it has regal colour, elegant black-cherry-cassis mineral fruit already developing and is really quite special; 14% alcohol.

🍷 9 Château Sénéjac 2020 £19.50
The rich maroon colour's so dense it could be black and the luxurious nature of this classic claret corresponds entirely: fruit-cake and cigar box nose, silky developed creamy cassis fruit ideally weighted and balanced, tastes very expensive and special; 13.5% alcohol.

ITALY

🍷 8 Marchesini Rosso 2023 £7.85
Smart-looking generic Piedmont wine by reliable Fratelli Martini bouncing with brambly barbera fruit, juicily vigorous and thoroughly Italian, complete with proper nutskin-dry finish; 13.5% alcohol. Perfect pasta partner.

🍷 8 Vanita Negroamaro 2022 £8.95
Gripping Puglia wine from indigenous negroamaro grape; intensely coloured and ripely rounded in black fruit in the best southern Italian tradition, complete with orotund heraldic-style label; 13.5% alcohol.

🍷 10 Palladino Molise Biferno Riserva 2019 £9.50
Eternal favourite from the obscure DOC of Molise south of the Abruzzi and as arrestingly delicious as ever in this new vintage, intense in its pruny-blackberry fruit with notes of black pepper, mint, clove and raisin cannily enriched with time in oak but balanced by an eager bite of acidity and clench of ripe tannin; 13.5% alcohol. It is by no means stocked in every Co-op, but go online to find your nearest outlet that does.

RED WINES

ITALY

🍷 8 **Poggio Baddiola 2021** £12.00

A sort of everyday 'supertuscan' from Chianti country, it's two-thirds sangiovese, the Chianti grape, and one-third Bordeaux grapes merlot and petit verdot, all aged 10 months in French barriques emerging as a sort of Italian claret and none the worse for that: plump cherry-cassis style with lusciousness and length; 13% alcohol.

PORTUGAL

🍷 8 **Sedoso 2021** £8.50

New one to me, in a quaint black bottle with painted-on-style naming, this is from Port country and entirely from the grape varieties that go into the fortified wine. But this is counterintuitively light in colour and weight, unoaked and just 11% alcohol. I liked it just the same: vivid berry fruits in a firm texture, wholesome, reassuringly crafted.

SOUTH AFRICA

🍷 9 **Zalze Shiraz Grenache Cabernet Franc Fairtrade 2022** £8.75

Substantial blend from Kleine Zalze, a leading Fairtrade winery in the Western Cape, with a lovely jewel-like colour, focused blackberry-plum-warm-spice savours and oak richness, finishing long but very trim; 14.5% alcohol. Tastes special.

SPAIN

🍷 8 **Co-op Old-Vine Garnacha 2023** £6.25

From the utilitarian Campo de Borja DO next to Zaragoza, a sturdy bargain: toasty ripeness of black fruit with spicy tannins, a wholesome match for meaty menus; 14% alcohol.

USA

🍷 8 **Co-op Irresistible Californian Zinfandel 2021** £10.75

A surprise. You get the expected sweet slightly scorched black berry style of Californian Zin but in this case not the sugary cloy I tend to find. This one has relishable ripeness, likeable in weight and balance, and does have a character of its own; 14.5% alcohol.

PINK WINES

♀ 8 Co-op Fairtrade Shiraz Rosé 2023   £7.00
Salmon pink, dry but positively fruity, party wine from redoubtable La Riojana winery; honestly made and sensibly priced; 12.5% alcohol.

♀ 8 Artesano de Argento Organic Malbec
     Fairtrade Rosé 2023   £9.50
There's a lick of super-ripeness in this otherwise dry and straight strawberry-fruit pale pink from Mendoza malbec; 12.5% alcohol.

♀ 8 Casanova Corsican Rosé 2023   £8.50
Casanova is a quaint old village on Corsica sadly unrelated to the disreputable Venetian adventurer, but here's a nice flesh-pink ripe but dry and citrus-tangy refresher from the island's native grapes; 11% alcohol.

♀ 8 La Petite Laurette du Midi Rosé 2023   £8.75
Smartly packaged pale-copper edgy dry Languedoc wine with perky floral aroma and crisp fruit nicely balanced; 12.5% alcohol.

♀ 8 Co-op Irresistible Côte de Provence Rosé 2023   £10.50
Of 17 rosé wines kindly opened for us scribblers by the Co-op team at this year's tasting, I liked this one best for quality and value. As with all Provence pinks it's not cheap but it does have a fine copper-onion-skin colour and lucid, alpine-strawberry-trace in the ripe but aboundingly fresh fruit, dry, crisp and endearing; 13% alcohol.

♀ 8 Château Barthès Bandol Rosé 2022   £14.50
If you're serious about rosé here's a fashionable one from the chic Côte d'Azur village of Bandol. Fine onion-skin hue, floral perfume, full ripe fruits evoking pomegranate and redcurrant, very fresh and tangy; 14% alcohol.

PINK WINES

8 **Welmoed Rosé 2024**   **£7.65**

A citrus twist to the strawberry fruit gives wholesome balance
to this clean and decent Stellenbosch pink at a sensible price –
the first wine I tasted in 2024 from the vintage of that year;
12.5% alcohol.

8 **Co-op Irresistible Solo Pale Spanish Rosé 2023**   **£8.00**

Rather prosaically named but a decent light-copper-coloured,
just-dry, red-soft-summer-berry fruit party pink with artful
balance and 14% alcohol.

WHITE WINES

8 **Andrew Peace Chardonnay 2023**   **£7.00**

Good-value straight crisp apple-fresh chardonnay; has had
some oak contact and includes a bit of semillon for added
richness; 11% alcohol.

8 **Robert Oatley Signature Series
Chardonnay 2023**   **£12.50**

This Margaret River wine of appreciable weight and ripeness
is enhancingly oaked and in healthy balance; special enough to
warrant the price; 12.5% alcohol.

8 **Maison du Vin Côtes du Gascogne 2023**   **£8.00**

Maison du Vin seems an anodyne brand name, but the wine's
inspired: from 100% colombard – a grape once mostly distilled
for Gascony's armagnac – it has tangy aromas and crisp orchard
fruit perkily ripe and nuanced, briskly dry; 11% alcohol.

WHITE WINES

8 Co-op Irresistible Viognier 2023   £8.50
Fruit-salad Pays d'Oc by Jean-Claude Mas nicely mixes apricot and melon mellowness with crisp orchard fruits into an enjoyably dry and fresh food wine: seafood and poultry, salads and bakes; 13% alcohol.

**8 Muscadet Sèvre et Maine Sur Lie Château
de la Petite Giraudière 2022**   £8.85
Flagship wine of the Loire estuary, Muscadet should be bracingly fresh and green and this one fits the bill: very dry but not harsh, crisp but with leesy heft and the natural match for mussels and oysters; 12% alcohol.

8 Co-op Irresistible Mâcon-Villages 2022   £10.50
Benchmark Mâcon chardonnay: gold in colour, lush with mineral minty sweet-apple long fruit of generous weight and eager zest, made by infallible Cave de Lugny co-operative; 13% alcohol.

8 Paul Mas Picpoul de Pinet 2023   £10.50
From the ever-expanding Languedoc producer Jean-Claude Mas, a likeable rendering of the popular Picpoul theme with salty seaside aroma, gently ripe white fruits in the crispy tangy texture and lifting lemony acidity; 13% alcohol.

9 Co-op Irresistible Chablis 2022   £15.50
It's made by Jean-Marc Brocard, a leading producer renowned for rich, long-lived wines from each of Chablis' escalatingly fabled appellations. This entry-level wine has plenty of heady gunflint aroma and classic minerally Chablis chardonnay ripeness; 12.5% alcohol. Quite special, and fair value.

WHITE WINES

8 G de Château Guiraud 2022   £17.50
Left over from last year, a grand dry wine from a top Sauternes estate full of the grassy-pineappley-tangy fruit expected of white Bordeaux but with an additional exotic richness; lovely wine for grilled fish; 13% alcohol. Reasonable value for what it is, but £2 up on last year's price for the same vintage.

9 **Rully Montmorin Domaine Jean Chartron 2021** £30.00
Rully is a wonderful but largely ignored appellation of southern Burgundy's Chalonnais region, making wines often of great character and quality. Here's one: pure-gold chardonnay but lean rather than fat in the manner of Meursault and the like, made just to the north in the Côte de Beaune. This is beautiful white burgundy that will evolve for years in bottle and well done to Co-op for offering it; 13% alcohol. Yes it's expensive, but it's an adventure.

8 **Kleine Kapelle Pinot Grigio 2023**   £6.95
I suppose you can't blame non-Italian producers trying to cash in on the mysterious liking for PG and this generic off-dry effort from vineyards all over the Mosel and Rhine regions has its own floral style on nose and palate, decently balanced and bright and just 11% alcohol.

8 **Von Kesselstatt Mosel Riesling 2022**   £12.50
There's always something from the splendid Reichsgraf von Kesselstatt at the Co-op. This year it's a simple young riesling with an intriguing grapey-grassy nose and corresponding delicately nectary fruit with textbook Mosel raciness; fine aperitif wine; 10% alcohol.

8 **Co-op Orvieto Classico 2023**   £6.85
Simple dry floral-apple-pear-green-herb dry wine from the ravishing hill-town tourist magnet of Umbria; it's authentic and affordable; 12.5% alcohol.

FRANCE

GERMANY

ITALY

WHITE WINES

9 **Vavasour Sauvignon Blanc 2023** £11.50

There's a lot of Kiwi sauvignon blanc at the Co-op (just as there is everywhere else for that matter) but this is the one that sticks out for me. Extravagantly perfumed and with a prickly-fresh seagrass and green fruit style just slightly softened with lushness it makes a particular impression; 13% alcohol.

8 **Co-op Irresistible Vina Gala Rioja Blanco 2023** £7.50

New-style fresh and crisp white Rioja; unoaked but not without a lick of richness from the constituent viura grapes; pleasingly balanced; 12.5% alcohol.

SPARKLING WINES

8 **Co-op Fairtrade Tilimuqui Sparkling Brut** £9.50

Fully sparkling fizz from excellent La Riojana Fairtrade winery made with Argentina's national white grape the torrontes, known for its muscat-grapy still wines but here perfectly dry and fresh with only the most elusive, and likeable, notes of the grape's natural nectar; 10.5% alcohol. Fine party fizz.

9 **Co-op Irresistible Eight Acres Sparkling Rosé** £18.00

Delicately coloured champagne-grape (and method) sparkler from prodigious Balfour winery in Kent has slight but bright redcurrant pinkness of flavour as well as appearance, artfully contrived, stimulating and fresh; 12% alcohol. Made exclusively for Co-op and presumably limited in supply at a typical 4 tonnes per acre in English vineyards, the price seems more than fair. You need a kilo of grapes per bottle of fizz, so eight acres would provide a mere 32,000 bottles annually.

SPARKLING WINES

8 La Maison du Vin Crémant de Loire £12.00
Busy mousse and a beguiling honeybun aroma welcome you to
this nicely made sparkler from the Loire Valley. The lushness
of chenin blanc and lift of chardonnay combine to nourish and
refresh in a well-defined brut (dry) style; 11.5% alcohol.

10 Les Pionniers Champagne Brut £21.50
You can buy the Co-op's house champagne in 2,419 of its
stores, which must be just about all of them, including my own
nearest outlet, Castle Cary in Somerset, where this fabulous
fizz is regularly discounted by a pound or two even though the
standard price is modest. Named in honour of the Rochdale
Pioneers who founded the first Co-op movement in 1844, this is
serious champagne made by Piper Heidsieck, creamily foaming,
evoking the aroma of lemon meringue pie and bustling with
vivid red-apple fruit, deliciously structured and ripe, not at all
'green'; 12% alcohol.

8 Corte Molino Prosecco £8.50
I'm not a prosecco advocate but this one is a fair price and
tastes less like confectionery than most – it even claims to be
'DOC Extra Dry' – and has pleasant peary fruit with detectable
acidity; 11% alcohol.

FRANCE

ITALY

Lidl

 Modest selection this year. Lidl's wine people are concentrating, reasonably enough, on their 'wine tour' promotions of regular selections, usually from particular producing nations, on the basis of buy now while stocks last. To begin with, there were four wine tours a year. Then there were six. Now, I learn, there is to be a different wine tour every month.

Fine. If you shop at Lidl at least once a month, you won't miss out. But from my point of view, writing a once-a-year wine guide, it's not so great. I can watch the scores of wines that come and go from Lidl month by month but I can't write about them. Not here, anyway.

I have to fall back on the core range. The wines that are on shelf year-round. Trouble is, with all the excitement of finding a whole bunch of new wines every four weeks, the Lidl team can have very little time or resource to devote to the comparatively slow-moving core. And it shows. There have been very few additions over the last year and, I'm sorry to report, rather more in the way of deletions.

Never mind, because there's a great new Italian red this year, Vino Nobile di Montepulciano 2020, at £8.99. Montepulciano in Tuscany makes wines from the same grapes that go into Chianti, but posher. Some are good, most are very expensive. This is good and not very expensive. Deal.

RED WINES

AUSTRALIA

🍷 8 **Cimarosa Merlot 2022**   £4.15

Purple party red with brambly soft fruit and suggestions of chocolate and cherry; 13.5% alcohol. I do think it's helpful of the Lidl website to give the different prices of cheaper wines in Scotland and Wales, where the devolved governments have imposed minimum-price penalties to discourage alcohol consumption. This wine's regional price is £5.07.

🍷 8 **Deluxe Barossa Valley Shiraz 2022**   £7.49

Price is up on last year's £6.79 but it's still a good buy: very ripe blueberry/bramble fruit saved from soupiness by a tidy acidity and trace of friendly tannin; 14% alcohol. Definitely a barbecue red.

FRANCE

🍷 8 **Pinot Noir Vin de France 2022**   £5.49

This light but nicely integrated cherry-strawberry pinot from, I guess, the Midi, has brightness of fruit as well as the grape's trademark wholesome earthiness; 12.5% alcohol.

🍷 9 **Bordeaux Supérieure 2021**   £5.99

Bordeaux makes most of the world's costliest wines and plenty of overpriced ones too. I can just about see why zillionaires who must have 'the best' happily pay £100-plus for a famed *grand cru*, but I am forever perplexed that anybody pays even £10 for dismal generic claret. Here's the answer: Lidl's own 'superior' claret, which I admired a year ago and is still, mysteriously, on shelf: great colour, cassis nose and palate, nicely knit and firm at the edge, and it's cheap as chips; 13.5% alcohol.

ITALY

🍷 8 **Chianti Corte Alle Mura 2020**   £6.49

Nicely streamed sour-cherry fruit in this maturing wine in true Chianti style at a very keen price; 13% alcohol.

RED WINES

ITALY

🍷 **10** **Vino Nobile di Montepulciano 2020** £8.99
Remarkably complete and toothsome Vino Nobile at a giveaway price from the Lidl core range, it's sleek and darkly savoury with trademark Tuscan sour-cherry fruit, lifting acidity and ideal nutskin-dry finish; 13.5% alcohol. My wine of the year at Lidl and, I hope, a harbinger of things to come.

PORTUGAL

🍷 **8** **Azinhaga de Ouro Reserva 2021** £6.99
Admirably consistent core-range Douro Valley food red with minty-blackberry darkness and savour with a lick of porty vanilla; 14% alcohol.

SPAIN

🍷 **8** **Cepa Lebrel Rioja Joven 2022** £4.69
Lidl's almost unfeasibly cheap Rioja range kicks off with this vigorous unoaked midweight delivering bright juicy red fruit and tasting quite Rioja-like; 13% alcohol.

WHITE WINES

ARGENTINA

🍷 **8** **Alma Mora Reserve Chardonnay 2022** £7.49
Lush Mendoza dry wine showing the sweet-apple ripeness of sunny chardonnay to very likeable effect; stands out; 13% alcohol.

AUSTRALIA

🍷 **8** **Deluxe Limestone Coast Chardonnay 2022** £6.49
Big-flavoured, sweet-apple-peach unoaked dry party wine of honest merit at a keen price; 12.5% alcohol.

WHITE WINES

FRANCE

8 **Picpoul de Pinet Le Rocher de Saint Victor 2023** **£7.99**
Understandably popular Mediterranean dry refresher; it isn't exceptional value but scores for jangly-tangy zing and good intensity of ripe orchard fruit; 12.5% alcohol.

GERMANY

8 **Klüsserather St Michael Riesling Feinherb 2023** **£5.29**
Bog-standard Mosel riesling but a jolly decent crisp party wine with brisk apple fruit, a suggestion of grapey sweetness as well as prickly freshness, and overall a dry wine; 10.5% alcohol.

8 **Markus Molitor Sauvignon Blanc 2022** **£9.99**
New vintage of last year's unexpected introduction of this very likeable Mosel sauvignon. It's racy in the riesling tradition but very much of the snappy green-pepper sauvignon seagrass salinity; vivid and stimulating; 12% alcohol.

SOUTH AFRICA

8 **Deluxe Fairtrade Chenin Blanc 2023** **£6.49**
From the Paarl region of the Cape comes one of very few Fairtrade wines to be found in Lidl and a decent one: crisp opening to the lively chenin fruit moving between almost-green freshness to the nectar bloom that makes the balance, and trimmed by limey acidity; 13.5% alcohol.

SPAIN

8 **Cepa Lebrel Rioja Blanco 2022** **£6.29**
A pleasing gold colour and minty sweet apple nose to this convincingly ripe unoaked white Rioja; it's easily as interesting as pricier big-name rivals; 12.5% alcohol.

SPARKLING WINES

9 **Crémant de Loire Brut** £8.49

This creamily foaming Loire Valley sparkler pairs the crisp white-fruit freshness of its constituent chenin blanc with the grape's honeyed mellowness to delightful effect; a dry, refreshing party fizz of real quality; 12% alcohol.

9 **Montaudon Champagne Brut** £15.49

Stalwart of French supermarkets, this is a very respectable non-vintage brand at a remarkably low price. Inviting yeasty brioche first whiff, mellow style but brisk apple-freshness of fruit and lingering aftertaste; 12% alcohol.

Majestic

First things first. All the wines recommended in this section are priced at the discounted 'mix six' rates charged on purchases of at least six bottles from the stores or online. It's in keeping with Majestic's founding policy of selling wines on a wholesale basis, originally a minimum of 12 bottles, when it first opened in London in 1980. It was an ingenious notion: they sold more wine, and at a time of byzantine licensing laws, they could trade at all hours and even on Sundays.

You could say Majestic has never looked back, but it's been a pretty rackety 40-odd years. Right now, nevertheless, this remarkable enterprise is flourishing. There are more than 200 stores, an awe-inspiring online presence and a range of wines wider than at any other time in its history.

My little selection this year is a very partial representation but includes items from the burgeoning own-label ranges: Definition wines and the new affordable 'Chosen by Majestic' wines, which have impressed. I've noticed a new expansion of the 'fine wine' choice – a major Majestic feature that I believe stalled after the financial crash of 2009 – betokening, I hope, that good times are back for classed growths and grands crus.

Returning to the topic of price, the discounts for mix-six are at least 10 per cent of individual-bottle prices and usually more. I would earnestly counsel you always take advantage as some prices otherwise look rather high.

Majestic's strengths include, as they long have, wines from New Zealand – this retailer was a very early adopter and promoter of Kiwi sauvignon blanc – and from Italy. There's a lot of well-sourced Burgundy – not a commodity much in evidence on the high street or in the supermarkets – and as ever a fine choice of Beaujolais.

Grand wines from the southern hemisphere are numerous and exclusive, as is a large selection from the USA (where Majestic once had its own chain of upmarket liquor stores) but regional France is well represented too. My top buy is a nice dry white from the deep southwest, Duffour Père et Fils Vinum Côtes de Gascogne 2023, price £6.99. Mix-six, that is.

RED WINES

ARGENTINA

🍷 **8** **Trapiche Vineyards Malbec 2023**   £7.99
Bright young thing from a dependable Mendoza producer, delivering a lot of bold plummy fruit and ripe, even chocolatey, typical malbec grip at a good price; 12.5% alcohol.

🍷 **8** **Definition Malbec 2022**   £14.99
Grand, concentrated, smoothly upholstered, blackberry-plummy pure malbec from famed high-altitude Zuccardi vineyards in the Mendoza region's Uco Valley; 14% alcohol.

AUSTRIA

🍷 **8** **Von der Land Zweigelt 2022**   £9.99
Who would pick out this oddly labelled item at random from Majestic's burgeoning shelves? Zweigelt is Austria's native black grape, here making a cherry-evoking full-fruit plummy-grippy perfect poultry red of real character; 13.5% alcohol.

FRANCE

🍷 **8** **Chosen by Majestic Pinot Noir 2022**   £8.99
It's Burgundian-style pinot noir of uncertain provenance classified as a Vin de France, pinging with cherry aromas and juiciness, given a bit of gravitas with some oaked wine in the blend and a very pleasant light wine; 12.5% alcohol. From Majestic's new own-brand 'Chosen by' range and certainly keenly priced.

🍷 **9** **Château Recougne 2020**   £9.99
Generic Bordeaux Supérieur that exceeds expectations: well-developed blackcurrant and black cherry fruit is merlot dominated but has a measure of carmenère, a blending variety now near-extinct in the region and this might be the key. Fine claret at a good price; 14.5% alcohol.

RED WINES

FRANCE

9 **M. Chapoutier Belleruche Côtes du Rhône 2022 £10.99**
A Majestic perennial for decades, this is a sumptuous pure-fruit unoaked juicily ripe and complex wine very much of the land, with minerality, scrub-landscape herbs and warm spice deliciously threaded through; 14.5% alcohol. Chapoutier is rightly renowned as a Rhône superstar.

ITALY

8 **Nivola Lambrusco Grasparossa di Castelvetro £11.99**
True Lambrusco is a red, gently fizzing dry wine made in the Emilia-Romagna region of northern Italy, and it's hard to find. This non-vintage one is a good introduction: deep purple in colour, briar nose, tingling mousse, brisk brambly fruit, pretty dry and a top picnic red to serve well chilled; 10.5% alcohol.

8 **De Forville Nebbiolo 2021 £11.99**
Nebbiolo is the grape of Barolo, Italy's most aspiring red wine, and here's a déclassé version by Piedmont outfit de Forville. Limpid colour, clingy cherry-redcurrant fruit, some slinkiness from oak; distinctive; 14% alcohol.

9 **Domini Veneti La Casetta**
Valpolicella Ripasso Superiore 2023 £16.99
This might well be the first ripassso I ever tried, and it has always tasted quite distinct from the countless others that have followed over the many years since. The secret, it seems, is that the grape residue added to the must is from the making of recioto, the richer style of this Valpolicella style, and not amarone, as used for all other ripassos. Certainly La Casetta does have its own richness, a lovely purply intensity to its dense cherry fruit, with violet and mint, chocolate creamy almond; all poised and balanced finishing whistle-clean; 14% alcohol.

RED WINES

ROMANIA

♀ 9 Incanta Pinot Noir 2022 £7.99

Bright and fresh cherry-raspberry style nicely rendered for summer drinking – it will chill well on warmer days – from enterprising Cramele Recas estate run by English-born Philip Cox and his Romanian wife Elvira; 12.5% alcohol. This vintage has been on shelf a year, so look out for the 2023, due any time.

SOUTH AFRICA

♀ 9 Kanonkop Kadette Pinotage 2021 £13.99

Stygian maroon colour is the mark of this iconic Stellenbosch speciality from the Cape's native grape variety, pinotage. The roasty black briary fruit, smoothed in expensive oak casks, maintains the savoury theme but the weight is elegant and the finish trim; 14% alcohol.

SPAIN

♀ 9 Chosen by Majestic Rioja Crianza 2020 £8.99

I bought this vintage in 2023 for last year's edition, liked it and thought it would develop. Well it's still on shelf, turning out nicely thanks to sustained juicy-minty cassis fruit and evolving oak influence; 13.5% alcohol. Buy now while stocks last.

♀ 9 Definition Rioja Reserva 2018 £10.99

Another own-label Majestic Rioja rolled over from last year (see the Crianza immediately above) this has developed nicely along the way: plumply creamy wrap for well-defined juicy-minty blackcurrant-plum classic fruit made by grand bodega La Rioja Alta; 14.5% alcohol. And the mix-six price, bewilderingly, has dropped significantly from the £12.99 I listed correctly for last year's edition.

PINK WINES

8 **Definition Côtes de Provence Rosé 2023**   £11.99

Nail-varnish colour (well, depending on your taste) but a nuanced wine (by rosé standards) with noticeable references to nectarine and even watermelon in the fruit, organically made and daisy fresh; 13.5% alcohol.

8 **Agapi Kintonis Rosé 2023**   £9.99

The Greeks are getting good at pink wine, seeming to follow a formula of delicate colour, tangy citrus-led freshness and emphatic but discreet red-berry fruit and priced appropriately for the care taken in fashioning it all. Which is precisely in accordance with this likeable Pelopponese pink at 12.5% alcohol.

8 **Pasqua 11 Minutes Rosé 2023**   £13.99

Expensive but effective ultra-fresh delicately coloured and scented blossomy Veronese wine from a rightly renowned regional producer. It's crisp, pinkly nuanced in fruit and convincing; 12.5% alcohol. Eleven minutes is supposedly the time the crushed black-skinned grapes remain in contact with the must in order to impart the colour before run off. Well no doubt it was true in last year's excellent 2022 vintage but what about the problematic 2023? Exactly the same time? I'm lying awake at night worrying about it.

WHITE WINES

9 **Shaw + Smith M3 Chardonnay 2022**   £29.99

The winery is among Australia's newest, established in 2000, but is already garlanded with awards for burgundy-style wines such as this plumptious oak-fermented sublimely balanced maybe-Meursault-inspired luxury wine, very elegant and trim; 13.5% alcohol. Expensive, yes, but if you like burgundy but not burgundy prices, do try it.

WHITE WINES

**10 Duffour Père et Fils Vinum Côtes
de Gascogne 2023** £6.99
The choice at Majestic of wine under a tenner has narrowed
sharply of late but here's a nifty bargain from southwest France:
seagrassy-fresh aromas and fruit from a colombard-led blend
reveal reassuringly plump and ripe stone-fruit savours with fine
citrus trim; 11.5% alcohol. Gascony is a region to watch for
really interesting dry white wines at deflated prices such as this
top bargain.

8 Côté Mas Blanc 2023 £8.99
It's from Languedoc legend Jean-Claude Mas and exclusive
to Majestic, a lively grenache-blanc-led blend with orchard-
blossom whiff, peachy plumpness to the zippy white fruit and
citrus twang; 13% alcohol.

8 Chosen by Majestic Picpoul de Pinet 2023 £9.99
From Majestic's new house range, it's made by L'Omarine, a
good Picpoul co-operative, in a positively full-fruit zesty style
with touchstone salinity and a good citrus lift; 12.5% alcohol.

8 Viognier Paul Jaboulet Aîné 2023 £10.99
This florally perfumed dry wine from one of the southern
Rhône's great names artfully balances peachy ripeness with
grassy freshness to its basket-of-fruit complexity, finishing
bright and tangy; 13.5% alcohol.

8 Hunawihr Alsace Pinot Gris 2022 £11.99
The full name is Hunawihr Kuhlmann-Platz Cuvée Prestige
Pinot Gris and it's a powerfully pear-fruit, smoky, plump and
satisfying classic Alsace wine of memorable character, clean at
the edge but long in aftertaste; 13.5% alcohol.

WHITE WINES

8 **Trimbach Pinot Blanc 2020** £16.99

FRANCE

Trimbach is one of Alsace's most serious winemakers, but pinot blanc is the least-serious of the region's classic grape varieties. Try this lovely leafy-green, lush and herbaceous dry wine, plump with hothouse fruit but perfectly poised and fresh, and think it all over; 13.5% alcohol.

9 **Definition by Majestic Soave Classico 2023** £12.99

ITALY

Posh Soave by great Verona producer Guerrieri-Rizzardi, a very early pioneer in sustainability, is beautifully coloured with green highlights (I may be imagining them in my enthusiasm), lush apple-brassica-lime fruit with lick of blanched almond and fine citrus close; 14.5% alcohol. A classic Soave indeed except for the most unusual inclusion of 26% chardonnay in the blend along with the essential 74% garganega.

8 **Chosen by Majestic Marlborough Sauvignon Blanc 2023** £8.99

For the recently launched own-label budget range at Majestic this decent Kiwi sauvignon has been chosen from star Marlborough producer Brent Maris, known for the ubiquitous and inspiringly named The Ned range. Easy-drinking and fairly priced; 13% alcohol.

NEW ZEALAND

8 **Waimea Estate Albariño 2022** £13.99

I suppose there's a danger of Spain's distinctive albariño wines, from the north-Atlantic shores of the province of Galicia, being upstaged by imitators from other seaside locations, but this Kiwi rendering from the shores of the southern ocean shows competition is all to the good. This one has familiar salinity and tang along with its own sunny ripeness; 13.5% alcohol.

WHITE WINES

ROMANIA

🍷 8 **Incanta Chardonnay 2023**   £7.99

Genuine unoaked party wine with fresh orchard fruit, ripe enough to suggest hothouse peach and with a brisk acidity; 13% alcohol.

SOUTH AFRICA

🍷 8 **South Point Pinot Grigio 2023**   £7.99

A genuine benefit of the baffling boom for Italian pinot grigio, most of it dreary, is that further-flung producers are cashing in constructively. This Cape pretender captures the crispness of orchard fruit traced with peachy ripeness and has a citrus twang, as it should, and it's just 10.5% alcohol.

SPARKLING WINES

FRANCE

🍷 8 **Marcel Cabelier Crémant du Jura Brut**   £11.99

Full-flavour, eagerly sparkling chardonnay-pinot noir blend from ski country east of Burgundy is impressively ripe and yeasty with a crisp twang – nice variation of the champagne theme at a sensible price; 12% alcohol.

SPAIN

🍷 9 **The Guv'nor Sparkling NV**   £8.99

Very busily fizzing cava from an interesting blend of chardonnay with viura (the white grape of Rioja), some of it oak matured, has a little yeasty richness to complement the generous crisp green-apple fruit; very likeable; 12% alcohol.

SPARKLING WINES

8   Cune Cava Brut   £11.99

Cune is a leading Rioja bodega and until now I had no idea it had branched out into the Catalan domaine of Cava. This one is quite special, as it needs to be at the price (and it's £16.99 without mix six) with lush creamy red-apple and hothouse peach savours from the chardonnay-dominated blend; 11.5% alcohol.

SPAIN

Marks & Spencer

I am amazed and delighted at the number of M&S wines under £10 in the following pages. Value has become a potent mantra at Marks's – in the wine department at least – and quality is as consistent as ever. I suppose it's a not-incidental benefit of selling only wines made under your own name.

At this year's extravagant press tasting, more than half of the 100-plus still wines were priced at £8 or under and a good number had been reduced in price on a permanent basis as an alternative to occasional promotional discounting, which sounds brave to me.

Among my picks are plenty of wines from the recently introduced ranges M&S Found (wines from unexpected places), M&S Expressions (wines showing off the merits of particular grape varieties) and the premium M&S Collection. I must single out the Found Lucido 2023 at £7.50 from Sicily. Lucido is an island name for the better-known catarratto grape, once a mainstay of sticky marsala but now making excitingly fresh and fascinating dry table wines at keen prices.

A new Expressions wine I like is the Negroamaro 2022 from Puglia at £9.00. It's extravagantly oaked, organically made and, genuinely, a showcase for this emerging grape variety. My pick from the Collection is the new 2020 vintage of the St Emilion at £16.00. This is an unoaked claret of inspiring style made by one of Bordeaux's legendary dynasties, Moueix.

And finally to M&S La Dame en Rose Rosé 2023 at £7.00. I have awarded it 10 out of 10, the first pink wine to be thus honoured in these pages. Not just because it's terrifically good, but because it proves to me there is no need to spend any more than seven quid on rosé. Just saying.

RED WINES

ARGENTINA

🍷 8 **M&S Classics No 29 Malbec 2023**   £8.50

The vanilla from oak contact leads on the nose, flattering the darkly spicy fruit aromas and lending silkiness to the flavours in the mouth; a crafty contrivance I couldn't help liking; 13.5% alcohol.

🍷 8 **M&S Luna Dorada San Juan Shiraz 2022**   £9.00

Healthily ripe and balanced all-shiraz wine with appealing blackberry-fig-plum savours; 14% alcohol.

AUSTRALIA

🍷 8 **M&S Burra Brook Shiraz 2023**   £7.00

Lighter in appearance than might be anticipated in an Aussie red but it has plenty of bright fruit, evoking English cherries, a good weight in the mouth and trim balance; 14.5% alcohol. A pleasant surprise all round at a good price.

🍷 8 **M&S Classics No 37 Barossa Shiraz 2021**   £10.00

Inky and burgeoningly ripe typical Barossa bruiser with seductive spicy darkness of savour and controlled weight; 14.5% alcohol.

🍷 8 **M&S Collection Ebenezer & Seppeltsfield
Barossa Shiraz 2021**   £14.00

Pitchy-deep purple hue to this massive but sophisticated smoothie with long succulent savours revealing fruitcake and spice, and creamy blackberry-compote richness; 14.5% alcohol.

CHILE

🍷 9 **M&S Tierra y Hombre Pinot Noir 2023**   £7.00

Simple earthy cherry-raspberry Casablanca Valley wine; softly, plumply charming but trim and bright at the finish; 13.5% alcohol. Good value.

RED WINES

CHILE

🍷 8   **M&S Emiliana Organic Malbec 2022**   **£8.00**

Less sinewy than its Argentinian counertpart might be, a Chilean pure malbec with suppleness and spice in the ripe black fruit; 13.5% alcohol.

ENGLAND

🍷 8   **M&S Balfour Pinot Noir 2022**   **£22.00**

Kentish burgundy! It's from the enterprising Balfour Winery's pinot noir vines, rooted deep in the Wealden clay, and might just presage a new world of luscious English red wine. For the moment, this has an attractive jewel-like ruby colour, earthy raspberry aroma and recognisable pinot fruit, quite grippy with nice definition; 12.5% alcohol. The price looks mad when you think of pinots from the southern hemisphere you could buy for £22, but compared to burgundy, I suppose it's a start.

🍷 9   **M&S Le Froglet Shiraz 2023**   **£7.00**

Annoying nomenclature: not just the juvenile Froglet but the Shiraz. Here in Europe it's the syrah, and this Languedoc rendering is a good one: dense in colour and weightiness of warmly spicy briar fruit artfully balanced and wholesome; 13% alcohol. Good value.

FRANCE

🍷 8   **M&S Côtes du Rhône Pont de Fleur 2022**   **£7.00**

Light colour and body but firm sunny spicy recognisable CdR fruit with good definition – good value too; 13% alcohol.

🍷 8   **M&S Chez Michel Fitou 2022**   **£8.00**

Once the trailblazer appellation for the revived wines of the Languedoc, Fitou has been sadly elusive since the fading of its once-revered co-op Mont Tauch, but here's a reminder of the good times: firmly ripe hedgerow-berry fruits with a garrigue warmth and somehow very natural juiciness; good defintion; 14% alcohol.

RED WINES

8 **M&S Chez Michel Cahors 2022** £9.00
Beetroot colour, blackly fruity and spicy nose with a bit of black-cherry sweetness (there's one-fifth merlot along with the malbec in this mix) and a vigorous but poised balance to the whole, finishing with a friendly grip; 13% alcohol.

8 **M&S Chez Michel Bordeaux Merlot 2022** £10.00
Reassuring deep crimson colour to this young generic claret from Sichel (good name to follow) and sweet black-cherry merlot scent to the firm, bright juicy unoaked fruit; 14% alcohol.

8 **M&S Maison Riveraine Morgon 2022** £14.00
Morgon is one of the elite of Beaujolais – ten individual appellations making wine under the name of their cru – and here's a good one. You get the blue bounce of the gamay grape – source of all Beaujolais, however grand – in a generously structured and juicy medium with lingering flavours and marked tannins; 13% alcohol. This wine will keep and develop for years yet.

9 **M&S Collection St Emilion 2020** £16.00
Luscious successor to last year's launch 2019 vintage of this generic merlot-cabernet franc blend from Bordeaux's right-bank appellation St Emilion. True to the poised, terroir-evoking style of the famous AP, it is made by Moueix, owners of neighbouring Pomerol's apex estate, Pétrus. Lovely silky claret already well evolved and capable of mellowing further, say M&S, for up to five years; 14% alcohol.

RED WINES

GEORGIA

🍷 8 **M&S Found Saperavi 2021** £10.00
Very dark and dense colour from saperavi grapes which
have some redness in their juice (very few varieties do) and a
distinctive kind of engorged briar-spicy fruit in well-balanced
frame of savour and texture; good partner for richer pasta
dishes; 13% alcohol.

🍷 10 **M&S Montepulciano d'Abruzzo 2022** £6.50
There is clearly a glut of the fabulously delicious montepulciano
wine made in the Abruzzo region of Italy's east midlands as
every supermarket seems to have at least one, and the prices are
madly low. This densely-rich-coloured one delivers a dollop of
ice-cream-topping-type cassis lushness but is nevertheless brisk
and vivid, long in savour and very nicely trim at the finish; 13%
alcohol.

🍷 9 **M&S Primo Arte Primitivo 2023** £7.00
Fun spotty label attracts the eye and the wine, from Puglia,
delivers: bumper ripe black fruit fortified with chocolate and
gentle spice has a seductive mouthfeel and is a sure-fire food
matcher, finishing brisk; 13% alcohol. Very keen price.

🍷 8 **M&S Found Marzemino 2023** £7.50
Marzemino, a grape variety native to Italy's northeast, once
made red wine so popular it was featured in the climactic
banquet of *Don Giovanni*, Mozart's greatest opera, of 1787.
This revival is a light, spare red of cherry fruitiness, brisk but
firm and dry; 12% alcohol. It will chill well.

🍷 9 **M&S Barbera d'Asti Superiore 2021** £8.00
Inky purple colour in spite of relative maturity and certainly
mellow, this is slickly briary and intense with a crafty sweetness
at heart; proper tastebud grabber by excellent Piedmont outfit
Araldica; 14.5% alcohol. Good value at this 'new every day
lower price'.

ITALY

RED WINES

▼ 9 M&S Expressions Organic Negroamaro 2022   £9.00
Very dark opaque colour and a ritzy vanilla oakiness on the nose lead you into this luxuriantly ripe Puglian pure varietal with peppery notes and a well-judged weight; thoroughly Italian and very likeable; 13% alcohol.

▼ 9 M&S La Cascata Passivento 2022   £9.00
The secret here is the drying of a proportion of the negroamaro and primitivo grapes for this specialty Puglia wine before fermentation. It has a relishable sweetness, not at all confected, with dark notes of coffee and bitter chocolate; savoury and comforting; 14% alcohol.

▼ 9 M&S Fontenari Toscana Rosso 2021   £10.00
This pleasing blackcurrant/sour cherry Chianti-style blend has sleek purity of fruit really tasting rather grand – I was completely taken in; 14% alcohol. Special-occasion wine at an (almost) everyday price.

▼ 9 M&S Notte Stellata Primitivo
di Manduria 2021   £11.00
Manduria holds the high ground in Puglia for posh primitivo, as evidenced by this star-studded (far-out astrological label), extravagantly oaked sweet-tannin, ripe plum and bramble pure primitivo of lovely texture and savour; 13.5% alcohol. Worth the premium.

▼ 9 M&S Clocktower Pinot Noir 2022   £14.00
Fine garnet colour with brilliant clarity (it seemed to me, anyway) a textbook cherry-strawberry style from Marlborough's excellent Wither Hills winery showing off the wholesome earthy nature of responsibly-oaked Kiwi pinot to best advantage; 14% alcohol.

ITALY

NEW ZEALAND

RED WINES

PORTUGAL

🍷 8 **M&S Lisboa Bonita 2021** £8.00

Maturing Lisbon wine from a wide-ranging grape blend including Port varieties and syrah takes a very firm grip of the tastebuds with its bold, minty-clovey and properly Portuguese black fruit, full of interest and nicely clipped; 13.5% alcohol.

SOUTH AFRICA

🍷 8 **M&S Peacock Tail Pinotage 2023** £8.00

Distinctive wine from the Cape's own indigenous black grape; hallmark pungent spice to the warmly ripe fruit and a wholesome heft; 13.5% alcohol.

🍷 8 **M&S Kopras SMV 2023** £9.00

It tastes like pinotage but doesn't have any pinotage in it – SMV stands for syrah, mourvèdre and viognier – with strong dark pleasingly tarry and spicy fruit of well-managed weight and balance; 13.5% alcohol.

SPAIN

🍷 8 **M&S El Duque de Miralta Ribera del Duero 2019** £12.00

I did not admire M&S's El Duque de Miralta Rioja range this year – signs of drying out – but liked this 100% tempranillo Duero under the same brand. Quite austere but full of promise: lush spicy dark and creamily oaked in the approved style, and will only get better with time; 14% alcohol.

PINK WINES

FRANCE

🍷 10 **M&S La Dame en Rose 2023** £7.00

Attractive copper colour and genuinely pink-tasting (apologies if this sounds like synaesthesiac syllogism) dry Languedoc rosé entirely from black-skinned carignan grapes is wholesome, fresh and for once a perfectly reasonable price; 13% alcohol. My pink wine of the year for value and a statement that truly well-made and enjoyable pink wine does not have to be fancifully expensive.

PINK WINES

FRANCE

🍷 8 | **M&S Rosé d'Anjou 2023** £8.00
From the Loire Valley, it was the pink wine of the 1950s and
60s before Mateus arrived, and was subsequently swept away
by a tide of Provence rosé, but here's a reminder of the old
times: shocking-pink colour, confected floral nose, big boiled-
sweet flavour but technically dry with a relieving citrus lift;
10.5% alcohol. Pure nostalgia.

🍷 8 | **M&S Côtes du Rhône Pont de Fleur Rosé 2023** £8.50
Made by giant Cellier des Dauphins, a very decent dry style
with good fruit clarity and freshness; 12.5% alcohol.

GREECE

🍷 8 | **M&S Myrtia Moschofilero Assyrtiko Rosé 2023** £10.00
Grown-up (for rosé) Peloponnese holiday wine – bright and
dry but not without juicy red berry fruit and friendly freshness;
12.5% alcohol. Quite stylish, so the price is forgivable.

ITALY

🍷 8 | **M&S Found Susumaniello Rosé 2023** £9.00
From 'non-regional' Italy, according to M&S, but 'grown in
sandy soils with good drainage enjoying mild winters with hot
weather during spring and summer' a pale-coloured but full-
flavoured sort of rosé with plenty of residual sugar but not of
a cloying nature; 12.5% alcohol. Healthy sweetness, likeable
wine.

SPAIN

🍷 8 | **M&S Paco Real Rioja Rosado 2023** £8.00
Shell-pink apple-blossom-perfumed dry style with a nice trace
of redcurrant amid the fresh berry fruit; 13% alcohol.

WHITE WINES

Y 8 **Burra Brook Sauvignon Blanc 2023**　　　£7.00
As prices for Kiwi sauvignon escalate, competitors from
Australia (and South Africa) might just come into their own,
as this bargain from a winery called Free Run Juice does.
Zesty green style with grassiness and a little plumping (note
10% chardonnay in the mix) to partner the tanginess; 10.5%
alcohol.

Y 8 **M&S Lock Keeper's Reserve Chardonnay 2023**　£7.50
Artful party chardonnay fermented with oak contact for a nice
lick of creamy richness is one of M&S's 'new every day lower
price' wines this year, and jolly good value; 12.5% alcohol.

Y 8 **M&S Ya'Po Sauvignon Blanc 2023**　　　£6.00
It's from the far side of the world and look at the (new every
day lower) price, a perky gooseberry-juicy sauvignon of healthy
ripeness and cheerful freshness; 12.5% alcohol.

Y 8 **Tierra Y Hombre Sauvignon Blanc 2022**　　　£7.00
Bracing style to this Casablanca wine combining grassiness
with stimulating green fruit; 12% alcohol.

Y 7 **M&S Lyme Bay Bacchus 2023**　　　£15.00
At the price, this still white Devon wine doesn't stack up. You
can buy spiffing supermarket Chablis for the same money.
While our domestic sparklers are already firmly established and
price-competitive, the still wines remain a work in progress –
and surely deserve the support of the likes of M&S. So try this
one from the Lyme Bay Winery: it's bright, white-fruit-crisp
and has, dare I say it, an agreeable limey twang; 11.5% alcohol.

WHITE WINES

8 **M&S Chez Michel Muscadet 2023** £8.00
Straightforward bone-dry, lemon-tangy but not too acidic, Loire estuary moules wine of recent vintage at a sensible price; 11.5% alcohol.

8 **M&S Classics No 15 Picpoul de Pinet 2023** £9.00
Good of its kind, a well-coloured briny-nosed very dry variation on a popular Mediterranean theme; plenty of twang to the white fruits and keen edge; 12.5% alcohol.

9 **M&S Collection Chablis 2021** £15.00
Such a smart package from the elegant Collection range, another spiffy vintage from UVC, the Chablis co-operative that has been supplying M&S for more than 35 years. This is full of flinty aromas and richly ripe mineral chardonnay in the true style of this great appellation, perfectly poised and long in flavour; 12.5% alcohol.

8 **M&S Mathilde de Favray Pouilly-Fumé 2022** £16.00
Apex sauvignon blanc from the Loire Valley's heartland village-appellation Pouilly-sur-Loire, neighbour to Sancerre. This one glitters with river-fresh grassy-nettly aromas and savours, leesy and complex in its green and white fruits; 13.5% alcohol.

8 **M&S Tbilvino Qvevris 2021** £10.00
M&S have loyally persisted with this quirky Georgian confection for decades. In a throwback to ancient times, some of the wine is matured for several months in large clay pots called qvevris, buried in the ground before final blending. You get a rich colour, a dry-sherry-style aroma and likeably pungent dry slightly raisiny and exotic wine at 12% alcohol.

WHITE WINES

GREECE

8 **M&S Found Moschofilero & Roditis 2022**   **£8.50**
From the region of the southern peninsula of the Peloponnese known to the ancient world as Arcadia, a marvellous fresh dry white from indigenous grapes of sea-breeze zestiness, complex herbaceous aromatics and a sort of volcanic prickliness – very Greek, very modern, very evocative; 12.5% alcohol.

10 **M&S Found Lucido 2023**   **£7.50**
Made by Sicily's formidable Cantine Settesoli co-operative, Lucido is a local name for the island's catarratto grape, once a mainstay for sticky Marsala, now a flag-flyer for thrillingly fresh table wines. This one has lush stone-fruit ripeness counterpointed with seaside freshness, twangy lemon zest (lemons are another Sicilian speciality) and long, satisfying savours finishing tight and clean; 13% alcohol. Top Marks! A true find indeed.

ITALY

8 **M&S Expressions Vermentino 2022**   **£8.00**
Good colour, concentrated apple-pear fragrance and fruit, brisk but lingering flavours from Sardinia. You can sense the island breezes and aromas of the wild landscapes; 12% alcohol.

8 **M&S Found Manzoni Bianco 2022**   **£8.00**
Positively Italian flavours, I've written cryptically in my note, meaning I hope this mystery varietal from the Veneto glows with greeny-gold colour, gives off crisp aromas of white fruit and citrus and sings of freshness and generosity of savour, finishing dry and bright. And I believe it did; 12.5% alcohol.

WHITE WINES

NEW ZEALAND

🍷 8 **M&S Koha Pinot Grigio 2023** £8.00
PG fans might like to try this Marlborough spin, made to a low alcohol level of 9.5% but enjoyably balancing signature pear juiciness with alluring tropical fruit (papaya maybe) all conveyed with freshness.

🍷 8 **M&S Tawara Marlborough Sauvignon Blanc 2023** £8.50
There is such a proliferation of Marlborough sauvignon it's getting difficult to discriminate but I liked this for its tempting asparagus notes, beach-grass lushness and sunny disposition; 12.5% alcohol. Reasonable price too.

PORTUGAL

🍷 9 **M&S Classics Vinho Verde 2023** £7.00
One of many M&S wines this year offered at a 'new every day lower price' (the 2022 was £8 last year) it's a prickly-fresh rendering of the enduring 'green wine' of the Minho Valley and deliciously tangy, artfully balanced with residual sugar so it's not too green, and, yes, very fairly priced; 10% alcohol.

🍷 9 **M&S Found Arinto 2023** £8.00
This Lisbon dry wine from the indigenous but rather neglected arinto grape is a proper fascinator: good colour, sea-breeze freshness from the grape's natural high acidity but also from the Atlantic-shore location of the vineyards, and a sort of mineral-resiny strength of character that urges notice; hard to describe, very easy to admire; 12% alcohol.

ROMANIA

🍷 9 **M&S Expressions Feteasca Regata** £7.00
From Romania's flagship local white grape Feteasca, a very crisp but artfully ripe dry wine of real charm from a winery supplying several UK retailers. A very likeable bargain indeed; 11% alcohol.

WHITE WINES

SOUTH AFRICA

🍷 8 Journey's End Honeycomb Chardonnay 2023   £9.00
Don't expect honey flavours: it's a trimly mineral and bright
Stellenbosch wine with a controlled lick of vanilla from cask
ageing; balanced and refreshing; 12.5% alcohol.

SPAIN

🍷 8 M&S Classics Albariño 2023   £12.00
Workmanlike Atlantic seaside briny and forcefully fresh full-
flavoured new variation on the popular Galician theme; 13%
alcohol.

SPARKLING WINES

ENGLAND

🍷 8 Bramble Hill Sparkling Brut 2022   £15.00
New 'every day lower price' is a whole £1 down on last year's
£16 but let's not be mealy-mouthed. It is a breakthrough English
sparkler made by the 'tank method' that has so successfully
enabled the phenomenon of prosecco but this Kentish, from the
same grapes that go into champagne, is in another league. Very
perky and persistent bubbles, bakery whiffs, crisp white fruits
and tangy acidity; 12.5% alcohol.

🍷 8 Pet Nat Rosé Brut 2023   £15.00
Jazzy-looking item from Kent of the 'natural wine' kind, cloudy
in its orangey pinkness because it's not been 'disgorged' of
the detritus from the second fermentation. From champagne
grapes, mainly pinot noir, it has a lively sparkle, lemony
entry and distinctive orchard fruits with grapefruit stranded
through; 11.5% alcohol.

SPARKLING WINES

8 **M&S Classics No 12 Crémant de Bourgogne** £12.00
Pinot noir, the grape of red burgundy, leads the blend for this
charming 'creaming' sparkler from the region, and you get a
fine mellow fruit with lifting citrus twang; 12% alcohol.

8 **Champagne Delacourt Brut** £24.00
I think this is a younger blend than last year's mellow bottling
of wines dating back to 2016, but it's still very likeable,
appley-fresh with plenty of nuance and a convincing tiny-
bubble mousse; 12.5% alcohol. Interesting to recall that this
M&S house champagne was priced at £30 at launch in 2018.

8 **Finca Miguel Cava Brut** £7.00
Vigorous fresh full-fizz party sparkler from Catalonia; likeably
ripe and yeasty and certainly brut in style – refreshing and
keenly priced; 11.5% alcohol.

8 **Finca Miguel Cava Brut Vintage 2021** £12.00
Chardonnay-led blend for this grander cava from Jaume
Serra winery Finca Miguel ('Michael's Farm' perhaps echoing
M&S's St Michael brand of old?) teams creamy richness and
crisp white-fruit freshness in a very lively dry sparkler, mellow
and satisfying; 11.5% alcohol.

Morrisons

My local Morrisons seems to be having a staffing crisis. I queued for at least 20 minutes at a checkout one wet afternoon. It was the only one of 12 checkout points manned, and our queue snaked just about the length of the store. None of the staff hanging around the DIY-checkout points paid our complaining line any heed whatsoever. One fuming customer suggested we share one of my six bottles of wine (it was a multibuy offer) to pass the time, another worried out loud that her frozen-food purchases would have thawed by the time she got back into the car park, and a rather cross gentleman opined that the store staff held their customers in contempt.

The following day I read in the paper that senior positions in Morrisons' management have been vacated in dramatic numbers of late, since the appointment of a new top boss, recruited from French supermarket behemoth Carrefour. Apparently, he's known for an autocratic management style. Are these parallel staffing problems in any way related? I'm not sure what to think. What I do know is that Morrisons is owned by a giant American private-equity company. Let us hope it has a plan.

And the wines? Well, the shelf arrangements in store seem to me as random and confusing as ever, and while the frequent price promotions are very welcome, they can seem awfully complicated. Nevertheless, there are many good buys and good discounts and I hope the recommendations in the following pages will help you make a start.

RED WINES

▼ 9 The Best Gran Montana Uco Valley Malbec 2021 £11.00

Worthy follow-up to the splendid 2020 vintage, it's intensely purple-black in colour with a heady blackberry/blueberry pie (with warm crust) nose and corresponding fruit, very comforting, and briskly tidy at the finish; 14.5% alcohol. Made for Morrisons by the excellent Zuccardi family's Agricola winery.

▼ 9 The Best Barossa Valley Shiraz 2019 £12.50

In the 2024 edition, I liked this wine from its 2021 vintage because that was the one I tasted. This year, it's the 2019 vintage on shelf and I like it even better, even though the price has risen from the previous £11. It's a very dark, silky and cushiony wine with notes of coffee, chocolate and warm spice and the weight is just right; finishes brisk and lipsmacking; 14.5% alcohol.

▼ 8 The Best Chilean Carmenere 2022 £8.50

You get good carmine colour (the clue's in the grape name) and a generous heft of plummy-blackberry fruit plumped with oak contact and a friendly lick of caramel from signature Chilean ripeness; 13.5% alcohol. Comforting wine at a realistic price - I paid just over £6 on promo.

▼ 8 The Best Chilean Pinot Noir 2022 £9.50

Still on sale from last year this 2022 vintage remains a nice buy: quite hefty in style, good concentration of earthy, raspberry-cherry fruit with some oak rub-off but mineral and lively too; 13.5% alcohol.

ARGENTINA

CHILE

RED WINES

FRANCE

🍷 10 The Best Chinon 2023 £9.00

This bold new addition to the own-label range is from the Loire Valley, a glowingly delicious red from the historic town and appellation of Chinon, birthplace of Rabelais and high altar of the cabernet franc grape. This one has all the vigour and purply leafy juiciness that makes these unique reds so exciting, and it's lovely to drink now – try it gently chilled on warmer days, like Beaujolais – but it will also age gracefully for years; 12.5% alcohol.

🍷 5 Ambre Beaujolais Villages 2022 £9.00

It's about time Morrisons came up with an 'everyday' Beaujolais to fill the gap left by Raoul Clerget, the brand unceremoniously dumped a couple of years back. So here it is, at £9 rather than the £5–6 Clerget tag, and it's a let-down: flabby and dull, devoid of any resemblance to Beaujolais; 12.5% alcohol.

🍷 8 The Best Cahors Malbec 2022 £9.00

Plain-package robust wine from a deep-south appellation centred on the beautiful medieval town of Cahors; warm black-fruit heft from malbec, the local grape, blended with a bit of merlot to good effect; a powerful yet poised counterpoint to all that Argentine malbec; 12.5% alcohol.

🍷 9 La Quaintrelle Côtes du Roussillon Villages Lesquerde 2021 £10.00

From a remote corner of the underreported Roussillon AOP, a peculiarly packaged (pink label with stylised line drawing of a *quaintrelle*, a stylish woman) but perfectly poised slinky food red that emphatically needs decanting. It's ineffably delicious and I got it for £6.00 on promo; 13% alcohol. The 2021 was still on shelf in summer 2024 but I'd take the 2022 on trust.

RED WINES

⚲ 8 The Best Montagne St Emilion 2022 £12.00

Mostly merlot in this attractive claret from one of the satellite appellations of St Emilion it's already rounded in its plum and cherry fruit, nicely silky and brisk at the finish; 14% alcohol. Not cheap, but the quality is clear.

⚲ 10 Villa Verde Montepulciano d'Abruzzo 2022 £6.00

I've no choice but to top-score this because it's the same vintage I crowned in last year's edition. How come it hasn't sold out? To reiterate, it has intense crimson colour, sour-cherry-raspberry nose, juicily bouncing lipsmacking fruit and trim edge; 13% alcohol. The party red of the year, at a mad price. Again.

⚲ 9 The Best Negroamaro 2022 £7.50

Good new vintage of the powerful Puglian meaty-food partner, it has spiced baked blackberry savours with liquorice notes and clean dry finish; 13.5% alcohol. Price on shelf in summer 2024 was £7.50 and I got mine at 25% off in a multibuy offer, just under £5.70. But last year, this wine was priced at £9. Just saying. And one more thing: I tasted and retasted the same bottle on three successive days and it improved markedly all along the way. Dare to decant.

⚲ 8 The Best Primitivo 2021 £8.75

Robust baked-fruit Puglia wine of proper primitivo character: intense plummy ripeness with a trace of spicy sweetness, friendly grip from the tannin and satisfyingly long aftertaste; 13.5% alcohol.

⚲ 8 The Best Chianti Classico 2021 £9.50

Very decent plain-package wine by big producer Piccini with mellowness from a bit of bottle age as well as authentic grippy sour-cherry fruit; 13.5% alcohol. I got mine on a 25%-off day and noted how well it kept once opened – for two more days.

RED WINES

ITALY

🍷 8 **The Best Valpolicella Ripasso 2019**   **£11.00**

Ripasso wines originate in Verona, where they specialise in adding must from sun- or wind-dried late-picked grapes to new-harvest fermentations to give extra whoomph to the city's pale, light Valpolicella wine. This curious custom has caught on and you can now buy ripasso Valpolicella in just about every supermarket. Try this one for its pleasingly abrasive sweet cherry fruit and savoury depths evoking chocolate, coffee and prune; quite rich but finishing dry; 13.5% alcohol.

PORTUGAL

🍷 9 **The Best Dão 2022**   **£9.50**

Proper Portuguese light-touch but full-fruit juicy red from the overlooked Dão region south of the Port country of the Douro; 13% alcohol. A blend of local grape jaen with the Douro's flagship touriga nacional. I paid under £6 on promo.

🍷 8 **Pata Negra Toro Roble 2022**   **£8.00**

Ignore the cheerfully naff presentation – a cut-out bull-horn label emblazoned with medals including the Japan Women's Wine Award 2021 – and try this full-blooded blackberry and cream meaty-occasion pure-tempranillo red from the undervalued Toro region; 14% alcohol.

SPAIN

🍷 8 **Cune Mencia 2022**   **£9.00**

You've heard of Cune, brand name of Rioja giant CVNE, but Mencia? It's a grape variety native to Spain's northwest, far from Rioja, known for making Beaujolais-like, slightly tart but juicily fruity reds. I liked this one from the DO of Valdeorras: keen, unoaked, bright with raspberry savours, briskly dry edge and 13% alcohol.

RED WINES

SPAIN

🍷 8 **The Best Marques de los Rios Rioja Reserva 2018** £9.00

Convincing follow-up to the good 2017, a cassis-bright, creamily oaked boldly savoury wine in fine balance; 14% alcohol.

WHITE WINES

AUSTRALIA

🍷 8 **The Best Western Australia Chardonnay 2021** £8.00

Dare I say old-fashioned oaked Aussie chardy? You get plenty of creaminess on the nose from the proportion of the blend aged in oak but there's defined apple-fresh fruit here along with hints of nuttiness and even pineapple and a decided citrus lift of acidity; 13% alcohol.

🍷 8 **Fête de Flaveurs Picpoul de Pinet 2023** £10.00

Packed with flavours of lime with delicious hints of lemon blossom' the front label of this declares prescriptively. I don't disagree: impactful, tangy and very dry Mediterranean seafood wine, good of its kind; 13% alcohol.

FRANCE

🍷 8 **The Best Touraine Sauvignon Blanc 2023** £10.00

Big flavours: glossy green aromas and savours of crunchy sweet pepper, gooseberry and hints of more exotic fruits carried along in a grassy rush of limey freshness; 13% alcohol.

🍷 9 **The Best Petit Chablis 2022** £15.00

The junior of Chablis' four appellations can certainly equal its seniors for interest and value, as does this complex flinty-nosed, apple-crisp mineral and long-flavoured item; 12.5% alcohol. Perfect with fish and chips is the food-match tip on the back label. I'd take that with a pinch of salt. Prawn cocktail more like.

WHITE WINES

FRANCE

9 **The Best Chablis 2021** £17.00
The rather lush style to this particularly nuanced vintage has nectarine and lemon as well as trademark flintiness on the nose. The long, minerally fruit rolls tantalisingly around the palate; a marvellous expression of chardonnay from this unique appellation; 12% alcohol. The price creeps inexorably up, but the quality continues to impress.

GREECE

8 **The Best Assyrtiko 2022** £10.00
From Macedonia in Greece's gastronomic north, a fine floral dry wine from go-to grape assyrtiko. Peachy fruit balanced by limey acidity and long, satisfying aftertaste; 13.5% alcohol.

ITALY

9 **Morrisons Soave DOC 2022** £6.25
Morrisons' basic Soave is a stalwart, well up to standard in this vintage: green-apple-crisp and citrus-tangy on the tongue with a suggestion of blanched-almond lushness – Soave all the way – and a modest 11% alcohol. The 2023 should be a safe bet.

8 **Santodena Sicilia Grillo 2023** £9.00
Unashamedly retro labelling might be offputting but this grapefruit/orange-zest perfumed island wine is just the ticket: seaside-fresh white fruits of real zestiness as well as hefty saline intensity; versatile seafood matcher; 12% alcohol.

8 **The Best Gavi di Gavi 2023** £12.00
Aspiring dry wine from Piedmont has a slaking flintiness in convincing harmony with the crisp white orchard fruit, a class act nicely packaged at a slightly steep price (I paid £9 on promo, mind you); 12.5% alcohol. Very current dry Italian style from a good scale producer, Araldica.

WHITE WINES

8 **Yealands Reserve Sauvignon Blanc 2023** £10.00
Serious Marlborough outfit Yealands supplies any number of UK supermarkets with its bright and sherbetty pure sauvignons and this one does the job: perky gooseberry/green pepper aroma and crunchy fruitiness with good citrus twang and just 11.5% alcohol.

8 **The Best South African Sauvignon Blanc 2023** £8.00
Sunnily ripe in the Cape manner with gooseberry and tropical-fruit traces. A full-flavour, nicely lifted sauvignon of likeable intensity and balance; 12.5% alcohol.

8 **Capeography Co Cape White Blend 2023** £9.00
From a range new to me, the blend is chenin blanc with grenache blanc, marsanne and palomino. The chenin leads the way with honey notes and nectarine/peach ripeness and there's lifting lemon acidity to balance the oak-aged components; altogether enjoyable, dry and versatile; 13.5% alcohol.

8 **Séptimo Sentido Verdejo 2023** £8.75
A spooky label depicting a beardy messianic bloke mobbed by the forces of good and evil is an odd presentation for this emphatically crisp and briny dry refresher from the rightly celebrated verdejo grape; 12% alcohol. Séptimo Sentido, the seventh sense, is reportedly the capacity to choose between virtue and vice. Nice wine, though.

WHITE WINES

9 The Best Marqués de los Rios Rioja Blanco Reserva 2016 £13.00

Rare old-style oxidative white Rioja ageing gracefully into golden glory: canned pineapple on the nose, sweet-pear and guava richness trimmed with citrus, all enveloped but not subsumed in creamy oak; 12.5% alcohol. You might be offered the 2018 but it was this 2016 I found on shelf in late summer 2024. Worth seeking out.

FORTIFIED WINES

8 The Best Ten-Year-Old Tawny Port £15.00

Aged port is described as tawny when it's been matured in casks rather than bottles (as 'vintage' port is). The idea is that in wood the natural ruby colour of the wine gradually fades to what can be a very attractive coppery hue known in the trade as tawny. In this splendid tawny, however, you'll notice it's really ruby in colour. It's because it takes more than a decade for the colour to alter much. But what is tawny about this one is that it has the creamy sweetness and soft preserved-fruit savours unique to the wood-ageing process; 20% alcohol.

10 The Best Palo Cortado Sherry 37.5cl £7.25

Just one of three magnificent Emilio Lustau sherries in half bottles (there's also Oloroso and Pedro Ximenes), this is gorgeously coloured, pungent and heady on the nose and sublime on the palate delivering nutty-figgy-raisiny savours carried in a fascinatingly dry-finishing medium; 19% alcohol. Serve well chilled.

Morrisons

SPARKLING WINES

⏛ 9 The Best English Sparkling Grand Reserve Brut   £24.00
Elusive house English sparkler with a new description - 'Grand Reserve' has positively French pretensions - and this year is labelled as non-vintage (last year it carried the prelapsarian date 2010) but it is gloriously good just the same, and three quid cheaper. Lovely mellow but brightly fresh full-flow mousse that has spent six years on its lees before disgorging; 11.5% alcohol.

⏛ 8 The Best Champagne Brut   £21.00
Last year, this house fizz was made by champagne house Boizel and cost £27. Now we're back to former supplier Louis Kremer's creamy and pleasantly yeasty non-vintage sparkler, nicely made with a lifting citrus edge and 12% alcohol. And the price is back on track too.

⏛ 8 Champagne Charles Clément Brut   £25.00
New to me last year, this non-vintage pinot noir led sparkler continues to impress with its bready aroma, ethereal weight and lemon-tang acidity; 12.5% alcohol.

⏛ 8 The Best Marques de los Rios
**   Vintage Cava Brut   £7.50**
Fully sparkling crisp-apple fruit with mellow bakery aromas in this fine cava from Catalan producer Segura Vidas; satisfying and affordable; 12% alcohol.

Sainsbury's

 Sainsbury's came up with a new promo method in the past year focusing on its Taste the Difference wines – easily the cream of the entire range – offering 25% off the purchase of any three or more TTD bottles. These deals have continued for weeks at a time, and I fervently look forward to their continuing to do so.

I have to say this is the only really good bit of news I have this year concerning Sainsbury's wines. Overall, the choice seems to be continuing to shrink and while, like in other retailers, wines with lower-alcohol levels are on the rise, so to speak, in line with the excise duty graduation coming into play in 2025, there is little else to report. I am not invited to taste Sainsbury's wines but do keep an eye on a couple of stores. There are still good wines on the shelves, and I am pleased to recommend the best buys here.

RED WINES

ARGENTINA

🍷 8 **Dada Art 391 Malbec 2023**   £9.00
Mysteriously named for the silly Dada (French for hobby-horse) movement of the early 20th century mocking the conventions of art, literature, cinema and who knows what else, this is a perfectly conventional malbec nicely oaked and sheeny with pruny-black berry savours; 12.5% alcohol. Certainly an eye-catching package, I got mine for £7.50 on promo.

🍷 9 **Alamos Malbec 2022**   £9.75
By prestigious Mendoza producer Catena Zapata, an understated-looking package but a pure varietal of tastebud-grabbing silky sour-cherry/blueberry fruit of seductive plumpness that clearly stands out from the malbec crowd; 13.5% alcohol.

FRANCE

🍷 9 **Taste the Difference Ventoux 2021**   £10.50
Absolute stalwart red from a very distinctive Rhône outpost centred on the volcano-like Mont Ventoux, known as one of the scariest ascents of the Tour de France and making wine with their own bit of brimstone spice amid the intensely ripe and concentrated black fruits of grenache and syrah. This vintage is particularly savoury and gripping; 14.5% alcohol.

🍷 8 **Taste the Difference Beaujolais Supérieur 2022**   £11.00
I'm struggling to become accustomed to paying more than a tenner for generic Beaujolais, even with the variably meaningful 'Villages' designation but this one is probably worth it. Consistently full-bottomed purply fruit bomb with juiciness and bounce, good in this new vintage; 13% alcohol.

RED WINES

FRANCE

🍷 9 **Taste the Difference Château St-Hilaire
Les Bouysses Cahors 2020** £13.50

The 2020 vintage is still on shelf and on last tasting getting better and better: silky, dark-as-night black fruits with artful oaking and long, succulent savours; 13.5% alcohol. Pure malbec (the grape is known as 'cot' in its ancestral home of Cahors from a domaine that started production in 1230.

GERMANY

🍷 9 **Taste the Difference Rheinhessen
Pinot Noir 2022** £8.75

It must be a decade since Sainsbury's introduced this most unusual German burgundy-style red and it's a good sign it persists. Pale but glowing pinot noir colour, crunchy-fresh raspberry-cherry fruit with a pomegranate note and a wholesome earthiness to the light but firm texture; 12.5% alcohol.

ITALY

🍷 8 **Taste the Difference Montepulciano
d'Abruzzo 2022** £7.50

Bouncy-brambly vigour to the fore in this juicily typical pasta wine from Italy's east midlands. It's generously ripe and substantial too; 14% alcohol.

🍷 8 **Terre de Faiano Organic Nero di Troia 2022** £9.50

Dense Puglia pure varietal with warm briar-prune fruit saved from soupiness by firm acidity – a robust contrivance from what must have been very ripe grapes in this vintage; 13.5% alcohol. Equally good match for grills and roasts and rich pasta dishes.

RED WINES

ITALY

Y 9 **Taste the Difference Amarone 2020**   £20.00
Burly but balanced speciality Valpolicella (see glossary p167)
is notably wholesome in this new vintage – chocolate/vanilla-
robed deeply plummy ripe brambly fruit with alluring abrasion
and plenty of poise; 14.5% alcohol. Expensive but I got mine
for £15 on promo.

PORTUGAL

Y 8 **Taste the Difference Lisboa 2022**   £7.50
Rather plush from oak contact, a bargain all-round menu-
matcher from the wide Lisbon region with intense dark fruit
and trademark clove-mocha Portuguese spiciness; 13.5%
alcohol. Constituent grapes include Port varieties and some
syrah. Impressive, especially at the £6.75 I paid on promo.

SPAIN

Y 8 **Taste the Difference Cepa Allegra**
    Rioja Reserva 2019   £10.00
Dependable perennial among Sainsbury's remarkably extensive
Rioja selection is sleek and satisfying in this maturing vintage
and good value at the £7.50 I paid for it on the now-regular
25% off any 3 TTD wines promo; 13.5% alcohol.

Y 8 **Taste the Difference CVNE**
    Rioja Gran Reserva 2016   £15.00
Dark intense maturing Rioja at the top of Sainsbury's wide
range from the region; mineral in its cassis and clove, sweetly
oaked savours, grippy and poised; 14% alcohol. Regularly on
promo.

PINK WINES

8   **Taste the Difference Fronton Negrette Rosé 2022**   **£8.50**
Safe bet from little-known Frontonnais region of SW France, it
has fine coppery colour and an endearing softness of hothouse
fruit lifted by brisk freshness and tangy acidity; 12% alcohol.
Negrette grapes mostly make Fronton's elusive light red wines,
and this rosy variation looks to me a better application.

8   **Taste the Difference Discovery**
Collection Bandol Rosé 2022   **£16.00**
Bandol is a chic Côte d'Azur seaside resort and home to some
fabulously good wines. Prices for anything with the name
Bandol on it are invariably high, and this is no exception, but
it's a grand rosé for all that: strong onion-skin copper colour,
bright raspberry-strawberry nose, glitteringly pure ethereally
weighted fruit, excitingly refreshing; 13% alcohol.

WHITE WINES

8   **Taste the Difference Barossa Chardonnay 2022**   **£8.50**
Made by Chateau Tanunda (a pioneer winery founded in 1890)
an enduring bargain: lush, part-oaked, healthily ripe apple/
apricot fruit with good mineral backbone and a correcting
citrus lift; 13% alcohol.

8   **Taste the Difference Bordeaux**
Sauvignon Blanc 2023   **£8.00**
Bordeaux sauvignon might have been rather swamped by the
competition from the southern hemisphere but here's a reminder
of the pure-fruit savours and delicate balance that long ago
made it the world's coolest dry white; crisply bright, poised
green fruit, lime and even grapefruit twang; 12% alcohol.

WHITE WINES

9 **Taste the Difference Jurançon Sec 2021** £9.00

Still on shelf from last year, this thrilling dry wine from between Lourdes and the Pyrenees is particularly attractive in colour and generous in fruit in the 2021 vintage. Worth seeking out while it lasts for its shining balance between apple-peach fruits with honey notes and zinging necarine-citrus acidity; 13% alcohol.

8 **Taste the Difference Côtes du Rhône Blanc 2022** £9.00

Also left on shelf from last year but up from £8 to £9, it's generously coloured, daisy fresh and constructed of harmonious flavours of hothouse peach, sweet nut and preserved fruits; 13% alcohol. Made by clever Perrins.

8 **Taste the Difference Discovery Collection Luberon 2023** £12.00

The Discovery Collection is Sainsbury's answer to the likes of M&S's 'Found' range of wines from unexpected places but it's a long way behind in the quest for the moment. This dry wine from the Luberon massif of the Rhône/Provence is pretty special though, balancing racy green saline grassy aromas and flavour highlights with sun-baked herbal essence, nectar and sweet blanched nuts, all twanging with citrus acidity; 13.5% alcohol.

8 **Laurent Miquel Albarino Lagrasse 2023** £12.50

Albarino, the grape behind Spain's rightly loved Rias Baixas Atlantic-coast wines, is deliciously manifested in this Mediterranean-France variation from enterprising grower-merchant Laurent Miquel's groundbreaking vineyard in the picturesque mountain commune of Lagrasse. Limpid dry wine with alluring grapefruit aromas, startlingly pure, even mineral, peach-nectarine fruit and a lime twang at the edge; 12% alcohol.

WHITE WINES

FRANCE

8 La Terrasse Chablis 2022 £16.00

I bought this anonymous-seeming brand on a generous discount from what seemed an elevated price and was mightily impressed. Great big flinty wine of expansive and almost preternaturally Chablis-style chardonnay, crisp-appley but nutty rich and fascinatingly mineral; 12.5% alcohol.

GERMANY

8 Sturmwolken Riesling 2022 £8.00

Steely but plush Rheinpfalz pure varietal, it has attractive aromas of sweet apple with a suggestion of petrol (good sign in riesling) and crisp zingy fruit, good weight and pretty dry; 11% alcohol. *Sturmwolken*, storm clouds, we are told, recall the lightning that struck the original medieval winemaker, Rheinhold, inspiring him to great things in his vineyard. Ho hum.

ITALY

10 Taste the Difference Sicilia Grillo 2023 £8.75

Aromas that might make you imagine a bower of jasmine and citrus shading a Sicilian seaside trattoria's terrace and a rush of crisp white fruits twangy with lemon freshness across the palate make this a positively atmospheric dry white wine with developing exotic flavours – guava and mango – along the way; 13% alcohol.

NEW ZEALAND

**8 Taste the Difference Marlborough
Sauvignon Blanc 2023** £8.50

Here's a Kiwi sauvignon with a difference indeed: it's from Sainsbury's lower-strength range with a modest 9.5% alcohol, and it's really perfectly good. Good grassy style with generous but zesty green fruit and a citrus twang.

WHITE WINES

NEW ZEALAND

🍷 8 **Taste the Difference Pinot Gris 2022** £9.00

Unnervingly close to the Alsace method with pinot gris, this is aromatic, smoky and herbaceous, a natural match for highly flavoured Asian dishes (just as Alsace wines are) but a fine aperitif in its own right. Good balance between exotic savour and brisk dryness; 13% alcohol.

SPAIN

🍷 9 **Taste the Difference Marques de Almeida Albariño 2022** £11.00

This big, bold, briny dry wine from a family-owned estate in the Atlantic-coast region of Rias Baixas was, I believe, the first supermarket-own-brand of this formidably delicious and distinctive wine style. Well done Sainsbury's for persisting with it across the decades. This vintage has big colour, wild aromas of lush seagrass and peachy ripeness delivering delightfully paired white-fruit fleshiness and twangy zest; 12.5% alcohol. Top seafood match.

USA

🍷 8 **Taste the Difference California Chardonnay 2021** £12.00

Pricy blend with viognier and grenache blanc, appropriately opulent in colour, weight and vanilla oakiness as well as peachy-creamy fruit, brash in the Californian way but not without blingy charm; 14.5% alcohol.

SPARKLING WINES

FRANCE

🍷 8 **Taste the Difference Crémant d'Alsace** £11.50

From pinots blanc and gris grapes, you get a fleeting suggestion of the lush Alsace style in this perky sparkler; 12% alcohol.

SPARKLING WINES

♛ 8 **Sainsbury's Demi-Sec Champagne** **£22.00**

Demi-Sec or half-dry could sound like sweet, but not in champagne. DS signifies the wine is not *brut*, the dry style adopted by the champenois for the British market in the 19th century and now dominant in all markets. This revivalist bottling by Louis Kremer, who also make Sainsbury's own brut champagne, is really only fractionally more dry; it's more mellow, less 'green' and still very much champagne. If you like yours a wee bit less challenging, do try this one; 12% alcohol.

Tesco

It was the supermarket wine tasting of the year: 139 wines, 23 of them new to the range, and while 'this is only a snapshot of the total wine range' in Tesco's own words it makes it entirely clear that our leading supermarket takes its wine offering seriously.

I hardly know where to start but should point out at once that if you are or plan to be a Tesco wine customer you had better get a Clubcard. Every price promotion on wines – and there are always price promotions on wines – seems now to be exclusive to Clubcard holders. It's not difficult to get one (even this tech-bewildered reporter is among the 12 million UK members) and it's certainly not difficult to use.

Tesco's wine range runs to somewhere near 700 different lines. Among the supermarkets it's second only to Waitrose in number, and maybe this explains the unexpected proportion of top scores I've discovered I have given to Tesco this year – nine, which is equal to Waitrose's total. I mention this because it's the first time in 21 successive editions of *The Best Wines in the Supermarkets* that any of its rivals have come anywhere near Waitrose in this respect. Definitely a sign of the times.

Among the Tesco picks is a humble non-vintage red from Chile, Lateral Pinot Noir. The price, £4.39, is incomprehensible, but the abounding vigorous appeal of the wine, the very essence of its constituent grape, is all too easy to grasp.

It shouldn't be too difficult to apprehend the merit of another top-scoring red, Finest Margaux 2019 at the rather higher price of £24.00. It's made for Tesco at Margaux classed-growth Château Boyd-Cantenac, and I believe it's very close to the *grand vin* itself, which costs a lot more. It's a sadness to me that the top clarets have been priced beyond the budgets of sensible drinkers and I think this fabulous wine is a very welcome portal into that disappearing dimension. Invest if you dare.

Back at ground level, I'm sorry to report that a perennial Tesco favourite, Finest Saint Mont, a bargain-priced autumn-gold aromatic basket-of-fruits dry white from Pyrenean France, has been dropped. But the mantle has been taken up by its Gascon producer, the fabled Plaimont co-operative, with a new wonder, Saint Mont Grand Cuvée. It's a couple of quid pricier than its predecessor, but it's a revelation.

One more. I was greatly impressed by the Finest Vintage Champagne Brut 2017 at the tasting and noted the price of £30.00. Suddenly that seems cheap. Tesco's Finest Premier Cru Brut NV is consistently delicious but its price has crept up to £25.00. I am emboldened to award the vintage wine a top score for value as well as sheer quality. I think a toast to Tesco is in order.

RED WINES

ARGENTINA

9 **Finest The Trilogy Malbec 2020** £13.00

The Trilogy is of three vineyards of the Andean province of Mendoza, the highest at 5,000 feet above sea level – which is very high for any vineyard – maximising the benefits of sunlight and clear air. Made by grand producer Catena, this fine vintage has wild maroon colour, rich black agreeably pungent malbec fruit and sleek oak lusciousness; 13.5% alcohol.

8 **Grand Mascota Malbec 2021** £14.00

Very dark wine indeed from Mendoza's aspirant Uco Valley. Assertive liquorice-coffee-evoking savours in the gripping blackness of the textbook malbec fruit, smoothed with more than a year in oak casks and mellowing nicely already; 14.5% alcohol. Will develop.

AUSTRALIA

8 **Finest Barossa Shiraz 2021** £10.00

Big but not overcooked classic: a plumply cushiony old-fashioned blackberry-plum monster of well-judged balance; 14.5% alcohol.

9 **d'Arenberg The Innocent Weed Organic Grenache Shiraz Mourvèdre 2022** £12.50

Such a likeable wine from a brilliant McLaren Vale producer, Chester Osborn, with quirky taste in nomenclature. Warmly spicy plummy-pruny black berry fruits bustle harmoniously in this discreetly oaked steak-night red with a well-judged tension at the finish; 14.5% alcohol.

8 **St Hallett Faith Shiraz 2021** £20.00

Premium Aussie wine is such a treat, and this special bottle from Barossa leading light St Hallett is particularly plush in its rounded fruit and yet clearly defined and balanced and, dare I say, old school in its refinement; 14.4% alcohol.

RED WINES

CHILE

♀ 10 Lateral Pinot Noir £4.39
Maybe it's just me but I think this is one of the wines of the year. Yes the mad price comes into it, but as bargain pinot goes, it's pure gold: youthful purple colour (though it's a blend from more than one vintage), sunny raspberry nose and bright, juicy, poised pure-pinot fruit, it's the very essence of the grape; 11% alcohol. Try chilled on warmer occasions.

♀ 9 Cono Sur Bicicleta Pinot Noir 2022 £7.00
Lush rush of new-squished strawberry-raspberry-cherry juiciness is generous in intensity in this elegantly weighted and vivid pure pinot, partly oak-casked and perfectly trim with savoury tannins; firm and textured and just 11% alcohol. Very good value.

♀ 8 Des Tourelles Claret 2022 £5.49
Yes, it still exists, claret at around a fiver, and this is a good one, deep maroon in colour, brambly nose, dark cherry-blackcurrant fruit and a defining grip at the edge; 13.5% alcohol. Mostly merlot by regional merchant-proprietor Yvon Mau.

FRANCE

♀ 8 La P'tite Pierre Rouge 2023 £7.00
Generic Midi brand by behemoth Les Grands Chais de France ('Europe's leading wine producer and merchant' says Tesco) this is nevertheless a distinctive blend of seductive ripeness and savour with notes of redcurrant and warm spice; 12.5% alcohol.

♀ 9 Finest Côtes du Rhône Villages Signargues 2023 £8.50
Quite a light weight for a serious wine made in one of the most torrid vintages ever seen in the Rhône, this nevertheless summons up the simmering garrigue landscape of the region with scrub herb and spice savours, plummy intensity and keen grip of the tastebuds; good-value ripe and friendly food wine; 14% alcohol.

RED WINES

FRANCE

⚓ **9** **Les Terrasses Saint Nicolas de**
Bourgueil Cabernet France 2023 £11.00

Very happy to find the successor to last year's introductory 2022 vintage of this terrific Loire red. Pure cabernet franc, it has the grape's signature stalky-leafy freshness to the eager brambly fruit, plenty of intensity and long dark, grippy savour; 12% alcohol. Very distinct style, a wine that chills brilliantly, and that will evolve fascinatingly for years if you give it a chance.

⚓ **8** **Famille Perrin Côtes du Rhône Réserve 2021** £11.00

From the busy family Perrin, yet another slick and seductive CdR of well-knit berry-fruit and spicy savour mellowed with oak contact and nicely complete; 14% alcohol.

⚓ **9** **Finest Châteauneuf du Pape** £21.00

I have tasted this blend of various vintages back to 2016 several times over the last year and liked it very much every time. Quite pale to look at, but of luxuriant weight and intensity showing all the benefits of maturity and the special ripeness of this great appellation; 14.5% alcohol. Made for Tesco by star Lirac oenologists Julie Rouffignac and her husband Gérard Lafont.

⚓ **10** **Finest Margaux 2019** £24.00

This is amazing, a superb claret from a classed-growth Bordeaux estate, Château Boyd-Cantenac, bottled for Tesco under the generic commune appellation of Margaux at half the price you'd pay for the *grand vin per se*. Unlike last year's 2018, which I thought needed years more in bottle to drink well, this gorgeously perfumed, succulent plummy-cassis-vanilla-tobacco prodigy is already quite glorious; 13.5% alcohol. Of course I don't know if it's exactly the same wine as that made under the château's own label, but I don't believe it matters. At the price, this is cheap. Really.

RED WINES

ITALY

🍷 8   **Finest Montepulciano d'Abruzzo 2021**   £7.75
Dependable juicy brambly middleweight pasta red has been available from this vintage for ages; take the next vintage on trust; 13.5% alcohol.

🍷 8   **Finest Primitivo Terre di Chiete 2022**   £7.75
From the Abruzzo, rather north of primitivo's natural home Puglia, a darkly juicy-clingy black berry pasta red with a plump of almondy creaminess and a neat dry finish; 14% alcohol.

🍷 9   **Aprimondo Appassimento 2020**   £9.25
Night-dark soupy sangiovese from Romagna with a proportion of concentrated must (see the glossary) is a lot of wine for your money, especially at the £6.10 price on a double promo. Very inviting pruny/sour-cherry aroma and big ripe sweet-briar vanilla-toned mouthfilling fruit finishing tight and savoury; 14.5% alcohol. Thank you, Dr Pat.

🍷 7   **Finest Chianti Classico Riserva 2019**   £10.00
Liked this vintage last year and it's still shelf, but it feels a bit dried out since I previously tasted it in 2023. Disappointing in a *riserva* wine that should mature gracefully; 13.5% alcohol.

🍷 8   **Finest Valpolicella Ripasso 2021**   £12.00
Boosted for colour and richness by contact with dried grape skins, this is Valpolicella-plus by Verona's excellent Cantina Valpantena. Bold red-cherry fruit with heft and pleasant abrasion, long-flavoured and finishing briskly dry; 13.5% alcohol.

RED WINES

ITALY

🍷 8 **Fonte del Re Lacrima di Morro d'Alba 2022**   £15.50
From the Marches of central-eastern Italy a quirky middleweight red from indigenous regional grape Lacrima di Morro d'Alba, vivid beetroot in colour, sweet rose-petal scent and light but firm sour-cherry fruit with a marzipan lick, very clean-finishing; refreshingly juicy and bright; 13% alcohol.

🍷 8 **Castello Banfi Rosso di Montalcino 2022**   £18.00
Rosso di Montalcino is the junior wine of the famed DOCG of Brunello di Montalcino, an impossibly picturesque hill-town of Tuscany where brunello grapes make the fabulously expensive eponymous reds. Cheaper rossos are made from humbler (but related) sangiovese grapes, as in Chianti. This one, from the American-owned Banfi estate, is sumptuous with ripe sour-cherry fruit enhanced by creamy oak and a bit of a treat; 14% alcohol.

SOUTH AFRICA

🍷 8 **Shallow Bay Cabernet Sauvignon 2022**   £6.75
This serviceable bargain is straight pure cabernet with plenty of blackcurrant pie appeal and even a dollop of cream thanks to oak contact and a healthy leafy brightness in the savour; 14% alcohol.

🍷 8 **Kleine Zalze Reserve Shiraz 2021**   £9.50
Very ripe near-burnt black-fruit savours in this unexpected wine. It's been matured 20 months in oak casks, most of them new, and does have the kind of de luxe creaminess you'd expect, but it's relatively inexpensive; 14.5% alcohol.

RED WINES

SOUTH AFRICA

🍷 8 Ken Forrester The Misfits Cinsault 2022 £10.00

Cinsault, originally a blending grape in France's deep south, prospers as a varietal in the Cape, where its ability to endure the hottest weather gives it a good potential future. This one has a distinct blueberry/fruits of the forest savour, defined and textured with silk and heft helped by brief oak contact; 13% alcohol.

🍷 9 Finest Viña del Cura Rioja Reserva 2019 £10.00

Spiffy new vintage of this perennial pure-tempranillo from impeccable Bodega Baron de Ley has sweet darkness of aroma and blackcurrant fruit complemented by creamy oak and balanced by supple tannins, already mature-tasting but certainly with years of evolution to come; 14.5% alcohol.

SPAIN

🍷 8 Finest Ribera del Duero Ebela 2022 £12.00

The positively glowing maroon colour prepares you for the strong impact of this friendly monster, still a young wine with grippy tannins masking the vivid cassis fruit. Last year the 2020 vintage from this producer, happily named Bodegas Portia, was nicely developed so the prospects for this are good, given a year or two longer in bottle; 14.5% alcohol.

🍷 9 Marqués de Riscal Rioja Reserva 2019 £15.00

Top drawer reserva from a grand bodega (est 1858 and now with the region's most architecturally spectacular winery), silky and plump even in its relative youth with clearly defined fruit and respectfully supportive vanilla from oak contact; sleek and long in flavour it's lush now and will surely develop for years; 14.5% alcohol.

RED WINES

USA

8 **Bonny Doon Le Cigare Volant 2021** £19.00
All credit to Tesco for championing the quirky wines of Californian one-off Randall Grahm, who specialises in Rhône-style wines at Bonny Doon (name after a Robert Burns song) vineyard at Santa Cruz. This famous tribute to the style of Châteauneuf du Pape is dense and plumply ripe, rich in warm spice including white pepper, and complete in every department; 14.5% alcohol.

PINK WINES

8 **La Ligne Rosé 2023** £5.49
Generic Provence IGP pale onion-skin-coloured bargain with brisk red summer soft fruits and a little lick of sweetness; a party wine finishing comfortably dry; 13% alcohol.

FRANCE

8 **Cave des Roches Méditerranée Rosé 2023** £6.49
I was attracted by the reasonable price: pale petal pink Provence unusually made with a good measure of merlot it has bold colour, a friendly berry nose and wholesome ripeness with a lifting dry finish; 12.5% alcohol.

8 **Arc du Soleil Rosé 2023** £10.00
This pale copper coloured pink in a smart package from the sandy seaside vineyards of the Camargue is made by the prodigious Perrin family and it shows: juicy strawberry-redcurrant fruit, very poised, brisk, defined and dry; 12.5% alcohol.

PINK WINES

8 Miraval Côtes de Provence Rosé 2023   **£20.00**
If you like a wine with a story behind it, try this one. The lovely
estate of Château Miraval was formerly owned by Hollywood
stars Brad Pitt and Angelina Jolie but they parted ways and she
sold her half to a Russian. The couple's disagreements continue
and are regularly aired in the gossip columns. Nuff said. But
the estate's wine is really good, singingly bright, crisp and
excitingly savoured; 13% alcohol.

8 Rosé Hola 2023   **£10.00**
Pale-petal Catalan pink from black-skinned grapes tempranillo
garnacha and syrah briefly steeped for colour; very dry, but
crisply fruited and fresh; 11% alcohol. Stands out from the
crowd.

WHITE WINES

8 Finest Sauvignon Blanc Semillon 2023   **£9.00**
The sauvignon-semillon classic dry white blend originates in
Bordeaux, where the best versions are delicately delicious but
these days rather overlooked. This Aussie version commands
rather more attention: fully ripe fruit showing keynote grassy-
tangy-exotic-fruit depths, full of interest as well as refreshing
qualities; 12.5% alcohol.

8 Finest Western Australia Chardonnay 2023   **£9.00**
Quite bracing in its crisp-apple zestiness – the 2023 harvest in
Western Australia was reportedly late thanks to an atypically
cool and long ripening season – this unoaked mix of chardonnay
with a tiny bit of chcnin blanc is noticeably elegant and poised;
12% alcohol.

WHITE WINES

AUSTRALIA

10 Tyrell's Brookdale Hunter Valley Semillon 2022 £15.00
Gold limpid colour lures you into this thrillingly pure dry semillon's mango-melon-pineapple savours in a dancingly fresh texture; just 11% alcohol. Wine of real quality by a famous Hunter Valley producer perhaps better known for mass-market brands, but clearly still capable of great things.

CHILE

8 Finest Valle de Leyda Chardonnay 2023 £8.50
Straightforward oaked wine with natural ripe richness balanced by lifting acidity, all with mineral freshness; 14% alcohol.

FRANCE

8 Finest Côtes de Gascogne 2023 £7.50
Sunny new label from this perennial party wine by excellent Plaimont co-op, crisp and tangy style to the white-fruit melange of ripe refreshing flavours; 12% alcohol.

8 Finest Floréal 2023 £8.00
Floréal is a new hybrid grape engineered to resist disease and thus obviate chemical treatments delivered by horrid polluting machines. The future? Well, this dry white from grapes grown in the Loire and Languedoc and classified a humble Vin de France is crisp, bright and refreshing with a nose evoking sauvignon and apple-peach fruit reminiscent of chardonnay; 11.5% alcohol.

10 Saint Mont Grande Cuvée 2020 £9.50
Tesco Finest St Mont, a favourite bargain of this guide for a decade, is no more, but here's a very acceptable substitute from the same Gascon stable, Plaimont. You get gold colour, a billowing aroma of orchard and tropical fruits and a lush pairing of red-apple and chanterelle melon juiciness, quite dry and crisp at the edge, and all with a leesy intensity that makes for specialness; 12.5% alcohol. I know I'm gabbling a bit, but do give it a try.

WHITE WINES

⚑ 8 The Pebble Sauvignon Blanc 2023 £9.50

Loire sauvignon attracts the description 'pebbly' in allusion to the kind of mineral freshness evoked by the great river's pebbled bed. Rather a good name for this new brand by Loire producer Fournier, then. I liked this nettly generic Val de Loire IGP for its grassy purity, lush greenness and indeed pebbliness; 12.5% alcohol.

**⚑ 8 Famille Perrin Côtes du Rhône
Réserve Blanc 2023** £11.00

As might be expected from the Perrin family, a sumptuous leesy lavish fruit salad of a wine, dry but luscious and comparable to grand white Châteauneuf du Pape (some of the best of which is made by Perrins, natch); 13.5% alcohol.

⚑ 8 UVC Petit Chablis 2022 £13.50

Fine plush Chablis with nutty richness in tandem with hallmark gunflint aroma and minerality all at a fair price (for Chablis) made by well-regarded La Chablisienne co-operative; 12.5% alcohol. The appellation Petit Chablis was created in the 1940s for new vine-plantings on higher ground within the wider overall AC. Any *terroir* distinction these days seems unlikely.

⚑ 8 Finest Mosel Steep Slopes Riesling 2023 £7.25

Nicely judged dry riesling with racy apple crispness and a measure of retained sugar in the sunnily ripe grapey fruit; 11% alcohol. Fine aperitif wine.

WHITE WINES

8 **Finest Passerina Terre di Chieti 2023** £7.75

From the Chieti province of the Abruzzo this dry, apple/pear-peach/nectarine wine is every bit as attractive as the eye-catching ornithological label might lead you to believe. The passerina vine is so-called after a kind of sparrow (as depicted) that likes to steal the fruit. Distinctive, lively aperitif or seafood matcher; 13% alcohol.

8 **Finest Pinot Grigio Trentino 2023** £7.75

Real interest here: a PG of proper smoky-herbaceous style, quite dry and stimulating; 12.5% alcohol. It's from the Alpine foothills of Trentino and has what I like to think is an air of mountain freshness. Made by regional co-operative Cavit, a name to look out for.

10 **Finest Soave Superiore Classico 2022** £8.25

Decidedly superior leesy Soave has fine gold-green colour, and a plump weight of orchard fruit enhanced by partial maturing in oak casks emphasising the trademark blanched-almond richness so well balanced by the citrus-nectarine acidity; 13.5% alcohol. This is the equal of some of the prestige brands of this Verona classic that cost twice as much.

8 **Finest Falanghina 2023** £8.50

Supposedly the grape of Falernian, the cult wine of ancient Rome (the label refers), falanghina is a revived variety now widely grown again in the ravishing landscape of Campania around Naples. This is a good one, gold and aromatic but dry, almost fino-sherry-like and twangy with lemon acidity; 13% alcohol. Perfect partner for scallops, garlicky prawns and clam spaghetti.

WHITE WINES

SOUTH AFRICA

NEW ZEALAND

9 **Babich Marlborough Sauvignon Blanc 2023** **£13.00**
Very pleased to see this new vintage from one of the pioneer Kiwi winemakers, the Babich family who fled conflict-blighted Dalmatia early in the last century for a new life down under and made the first modern-era New Zealand wine I remember tasting. It's a big green-fruited nettly wine of shining vigour and flagship quality; 13% alcohol.

8 **Cape Kyala Chenin Blanc 2023** **£4.29**
Cape chenin blanc can contend convincingly in the world's best cheap white stakes. This is an easy-drinking party plonk with flowery aroma, juicy apple-pear fruit with honey notes but comfortably dry with a lifting limey acidity; 11% alcohol.

8 **Mountain Vineyards Sauvignon Blanc** **£5.00**
Among many sauvignons kindly opened at the Tesco tasting this bargain stood out: non-vintage gooseberry-grassy easy-drinking party refresher at just 10.5% alcohol.

10 **Finest Stellenbosch Chenin Blanc 2023** **£8.00**
Masterfully made Fairtrade wine by Stellenrust (the maker's marvellously named as Tertius Boshoff) is at once nectareously luscious and zestily fresh in that miraculous chenin blanc manner and given gravitas with a good stretch in old French barriques; 13.5% alcohol. Terrific value for a very smart package.

8 **Amandla Our Future Sauvignon Blanc 2023** **£9.50**
From an all-black all-female venture called the Her Wine Collection, an immediately likeable nettly-nosed leesy and lively vivid grassy green-fruit wine in the best Cape tradition and the product of a very admirable team; 12.5% alcohol.

WHITE WINES

SOUTH AFRICA

🍷 8 **Rustenberg Chardonnay 2022**   £13.00

This perennial exemplary Stellenbosch classic is unoaked and made with wild yeasts (cultured/GM yeasts are the general rule) and I fondly imagine the elegant purity of this sleekly ripe orchard-fruit and almond-rich balancing act is thus derived; 13% alcohol.

🍷 8 **Casa Maña Chardonnay 2023**   £4.09

From the cauldron of La Mancha a cleverly made simple chardonnay by giant Felix Solis at a barely credible price; 11% alcohol. I entirely endorse Tesco's note that it's 'elegant, fresh and fruity'.

🍷 9 **Finest Viña del Cura Rioja Blanco 2022**   £9.00

Still on shelf from last year and none the worse for the extra time in bottle, an appreciably oaked (but not, sadly, oxidised) dry wine with luscious notes of sweetly ripe orchard fruit and a twang of citrus; 13% alcohol.

SPAIN

🍷 8 **Finest Viñas del Rey Albariño 2023**   £11.00

An old favourite with a newly styled plain-wrapper label (caught me out), it's another saline and serious rendering of the commanding Rias Baixas theme. Ripe but very dry with strong citrus twang to the crunchy white fruit; 12.5% alcohol.

🍷 8 **Mar de Frades Albariño Atlántico 2023**   £17.00

Just in case you were in any doubt of where the great Galician albariño wines of Rias Baixas hail from here's an ocean-blue tall bottle emblazoned with great Atlantic breakers to remind you. It's quite a package and the wine's terrific: glittering lemon-gold colour, ozone nose, strong tangy briny white fruit flavours, very dry and just short of fierce; 12.5% alcohol. A formidable partner for fish dishes.

WHITE WINES

8 Bonny Doon Le Cigare Orange 2023   £15.00

Followers of orange wines – whites made on their skins to impart colour and interest – should try this one from iconic Californian producer Randall Grahm. You get a bold orange colour, aromatic preserved-fruit perfume, healthy peachy-appley fruit with a fino-sherry-like weight; 11.5% alcohol.

8 Finest Albariño Uruguay 2023   £13.00

Who'd guess Uruguay? This is in the style of the rightly popular Albariño from Spain's North Atlantic coast, made breezy and saline and delicious by exposure of the grapes to wild ocean weather. It's the South Atlantic that invigorates the vines of Uruguay's coastal Maldonado region where the same vine variety now apparently prospers. The wine is full of lively white fruit in recognisable style and it's good; 12% alcohol. Nice try, Uruguay.

FORTIFIED WINES

8 Cockburn's Fine White Port   £14.00

Made just like red port but from green-skinned grapes (all the colour in red wines comes from the skins, as all grape juice is clear, please note) this is pleasingly sweet and fiery with nutty richness and honey notes but quite dry at the edge, very nicely made; 19% alcohol. An aperitif to serve very cold in a small wine glass or even with ice.

10 Finest 10-Year-Old Tawny Port   £14.50

Lovely glowing copper colour to this Symington-made wood-matured wine is followed up by luscious nutty-figgy-raisiny sweetness flamed by the ardent spirit in the happy marriage of well-fashioned port; rich, smooth, balanced and the equal to much pricier big names; 20% alcohol.

FORTIFIED WINES

SPAIN

🍷 8   Finest Fino Sherry 37.5cl   £7.25

Very pale, very dry and deliciously pungent sherry made for Tesco by Gonzalez Byass of Tio Pepe fame. I gather this is aged six years in solera (other finos typically do only four) and can well believe it; 15% alcohol. Serve very cold in a small wine glass but not too small.

SPARKLING WINES

ENGLAND

🍷 8   Finest English Sparkling Brut NV   £21.00

Convincingly made champagne-style busy sparkler from the picturesquely named Hush Heath estate in Kent is briskly fresh with red-apple fruit and a hint of pie-crust; 12% alcohol. Not cheap but it does undercut Tesco Finest Champagne Brut.

FRANCE

🍷 9   Finest 1531 Blanquette de Limoux Brut 2021   £10.00

Another terrific vintage of this stalwart Pyrenean full-mousse sparkler delivering creamy orchard fruit along a proper tide of bubbles; made the same way as champagne but with a dry, bristling style all its own; 12.5% alcohol. The date 1531 in the name is the year Blanquette de Limoux was reportedly first made – two centuries before sparkling champagne.

🍷 10   Gratien & Meyer Crémant de Loire Brut NV   £12.50

Gratien & Meyer are the masters of sparkling-winemaking in the Loire Valley. It all kicked off in 1864 when champagne producer Alfred Gratien (as the esteemed Epernay *maison* is still known) decided to branch out. This glorious *crémant* from Loire grapes chenin blanc and cabernet franc with a top-up of chardonnay is equal to champagne but different, burgeoning with fruit-salad savours topped and tailed with suggestions of honey and lime, a lovely 'creaming' summery sparkler of great character; 12% alcohol. Top value.

SPARKLING WINES

9 Tesco Finest Premier Cru Champagne Brut NV £25.00
The price has risen alarmingly, in spite of last year's scrapping of the punitive extra UK excise duty on sparkling wine, but it's still among the best supermarket champagne own-labels. From what are genuinely high-rank vineyards, it has pleasing gold colour, welcoming bakery whiff, full but crisp fruit savours and a very refreshing balance; 12.4% alcohol.

10 Tesco Finest Vintage Grand Cru
Champagne Brut 2017 £30.00
The leap in the price of its non-vintage counterpart puts this lovely champagne sharply into focus. I'd happily pay the extra fiver for the ritzily coloured, brioche-perfumed, mellow-fruited, sublimely flowing mature sparkler any day I could afford. It's all blanc de blancs – all chardonnay from top *grand cru* vineyards – aged for seven years in bottle before release and frankly I don't how they're doing it for the money; 12.6% alcohol.

9 Codorniu Vintage Organic Cava Brut 2022 £10.00
A blend of viura, the grape of white rioja, with native Catalan varieties xarello and perallada works magic in this lush orchardy creamy nutty twangy top-quality cava from Codorniu, not just the leading producer of these classy and undervalued bottle-fermented sparkling wines but the oldest family business in Spain, est 1551. Top party fizz at 11.5% alcohol.

Waitrose

A mere 100 wines were shown at the Waitrose press tasting, half the number of not so long ago. But I think this represents sensible economy at the upmarket grocer rather than any diminution in what remains by far the widest and most diverse wine range of any of the supermarkets.

During the course of the year, I have tried plenty of Waitrose wines other than those kindly offered at the tasting, and am happy to recommend more than 60 best buys in the following pages.

To start with a bang, I've top-scored Chapel Down Brut NV at £28.99. You'll have guessed it's an English sparkling wine. To me, it exemplifies the fulfilment of the UK winemaking dream: world-class products realistically priced. It's a project that Waitrose has loyally supported from the beginning, a generation ago, consistently stocking the best-chosen English wine range to this day. It's been a partnership between retailer and suppliers that should be the industry standard.

Waitrose deserves more credit than it gets, I believe, for the good value of its wines. Prices are by no means elevated above rival retailers and there is a nifty choice of 'entry-level' lines. Do try Heredad del Rey Monastrell Syrah 2020 at just £6.99, a robust but classy red from Spain, one of my top picks, which I bought for just over a fiver in a promo, and Blueprint Vinho Verde 2023 also £6.99, the best-value example of this popular Portuguese aperitif white I've found this year.

As a Waitrose customer I must confess to tracking their perpetual promotions calendar. Every month, scores of wines are discounted by up to a third, and from time to time for a week or so the entire range is offered at 25 per cent off on the reasonable condition that you buy six or more bottles, any mix. On a permanent basis

Waitrose remains the only supermarket to offer five per cent off wine purchases when you buy six or more bottles.

All this means that the shelf prices listed in the following pages are really for guidance only. For example, my perennial favourite Italian red Terre de Faiano Organic Primitivo at £10.99, very regularly discounted to £8.99, comes down to just over £8.50 as part of a six-bottle buy.

Don't overlook Waitrose's online wine service waitrosecellar. com. It displays the entire range in well-ordered fashion, offers the same promotional discounts you get in store, and lists a number of wines that are sold exclusively online – including a few of my choices in the following pages.

RED WINES

ARGENTINA

🍷 8 **Norton Colección Malbec 2023** £9.99
Opaque and chunky Mendoza pure varietal, partly matured in new oak and very ripe with spicy black fruits but it's not over the top either in style or price; 13.5% alcohol.

🍷 8 **Tilimuqui Organic Fairtrade Malbec 2022** £11.99
Made by leading Fairtrade winery La Riojana, a fine new vintage of this elegantly weighted and silky, vigorously savoury black-berry-fruit perennial; 13% alcohol.

AUSTRALIA

🍷 9 **Blueprint Australian Shiraz 2022** £6.99
A bouncing and balanced beetroot-coloured, oak-matured blend of fruit from several vine zones across South Australia, its generous black fruit is very easy to like, and seems cheap for this sort of quality; 14.5% alcohol. Nice house-wine bargain.

🍷 8 **Yalumba Vigil Cabernet Shiraz 2017** £28.99
Some of the vines for this epic Barossa Valley wine were planted in 1925. Who says Aussie wine's a flash in the pan? You get very dark blood-like colour, a big wang of cassis-vanilla-warm-spice on nose and palate and an explicit sense of heritage; very grown up and complete, probably immortal and truly fascinating; 14.5% alcohol. Waitrose Cellar only.

AUSTRIA

🍷 8 **Lentsch Zweigelt 2021** £9.99
Zweigelt is Austria's native black grape, here making an attractively purple, pinot-like squishy-fruit charmer of a red wine you might like to chill a bit for summer occasions; good weight and a crisp finish; 13% alcohol.

RED WINES

CHILE

🍷 8 **De Martino Organic Cabernet Sauvignon 2021 £10.99**
Saucily ripe and beguiling Maipo Valley pure cabernet, as dark in spicy blackcurrant fruit as it is in rich opaque ruby colour, slickly oaked but not overdone and endearingly old-fashioned in its generosity; 14% alcohol. Waitrose Cellar only.

🍷 8 **Costières de Nîmes Réserve du Palais 2022 £8.99**
New at Waitrose and a good addition for its rounded spicy black berry fruitiness, true to the style of this dependable Rhône appellation; 13% alcohol. I was alarmed by the polymer cork (never a good sign, I believe) but it's likeable and good value nevertheless.

🍷 9 **Remy Ferbras Ventoux 2022 £9.99**
Smart new styling for the label of this stalwart Rhône AC centred on the hill country round the mount of Ventoux happily reveals another very good vintage; darkly ripe and gripping with pungent savours; 14.5% alcohol.

FRANCE

🍷 9 **Saumur Les Nivières 2020 £9.99**
What a difference a year in the bottle can make to the best Loire reds. I bought two bottles of this on offer in spring 2023, opened one straight off and enjoyed the juicy but grippy cabernet franc tension of berry fruit with stimulating green acidity. A year on it still had the dense purply colour but the leafy-stalkiness had merged with the spicy ripeness into succulent silkiness; distinctly delicious; 13.5% alcohol.

🍷 8 **Esprit des Trois Pierres Costières de Nîmes 2023 £9.99**
One of several Costières de Nîmes at Waitrose, I got mine in an offer at £7.49 and loved its purply, peppery blackfruit vigour, true to the distinct style of this worthy (and worthily good value) Rhône appellation; 14.5% alcohol.

RED WINES

8 **Paul Mas Réserve Languedoc 2022** £9.99

Paul Mas is a major Mediterranean producer (est 1892) with a well-deserved following in Britain – current winemaker Jean-Claude Mas so values our loyalty that wines like this grandly bottled item from the 'Single Vineyard Collection' range have corks printed with the legend 'Mas Family' – yes, in English. It's a full-figure grenache/syrah/carignan blend of warmly spicy hedgerow fruit with dark depths and long ripe savours; 14% alcohol. Good value especially at the £7.50 I paid on promo.

9 **Cairanne Réserve des Hospitaliers 2021** £12.99

Consistent Côtes du Rhône cru (top village AC) delivering distinctive dark cherry-plum fruit plumped by oak contact and with enticing violet and clove aromas. I like Waitrose's note of a 'twist of cinnamon and nutmeg' in the flavour; 14% alcohol. Frequently on promo at £9.99.

8 **L'Empreinte Rouge Lirac 2022** £13.99

Lirac is the southern Rhône appellation most closely identified with Châteauneuf du Pape, only about 10 miles distant across the river, and making comparable wines at vastly lower prices. This one is almost fierce in the attack of its robust briar-and-spice fruit, intense and rich with firm tannins; 14.5% alcohol. Will develop for years.

8 **Régnié Cuvée Tim Domaine Pardon 2023** £14.99

Grand Beaujolais wine augurs a fine 2023 vintage in the region: deep blue-mauve colour, concentrated juicy gamay fruit with fleshy sweetness balanced by grippy tannin, lovely and fresh; 13.5% alcohol.

RED WINES

10 Château St-Hilaire Médoc Cru Bourgeois Supérieur 2019 £15.99

Holy grail: proper claret at a sensible price (even more so at £12 in a Waitrose 25% off everything promo) is instantly identifiable: alluring deep hue, lovely ripe silky cassis aroma with ritzy notes of creamy oak, elegant fruit of classic cedar savour ideally weighted (13.5% alcohol) and gently clingy finish. It tastes very expensive and as good to me as neighbouring Médoc estates costing several times as much. An experience.

8 Les Marennes Sancerre 2020 £16.99

Red Sancerre is always pure pinot noir and always expensive but it's not always pure joy. I liked this one for its firm focus of jiggly-juicy strawberry-cherry pinot with a nice creaminess and mineral purity; 13.5% alcohol.

8 Châteauneuf du Pape Clos Saint Michel 2022 £25.99

Surely a good wine of its kind but equally surely, a wine not yet ready to drink. It has dense colour, lavish aromas and well-knit complex black berry fruits in the best Châteauneuf tradition but it's tough, tannic and closed up; 14.5% alcohol. A good investment though; buy a bottle or two on promo at £20 or so, keep five years and you might well have a bargain.

8 Joseph Drouhin Côte de Beaune 2019 £38.99

Drouhin is among the top wineries of Burgundy, with 1er and grand cru vintages priced up to and above £1,000 a bottle. But Drouhin also enjoys renown for its generic burgundies of dependable – but exciting – quality for us quotidian wine lovers. Try this pure pinot noir from the wider Côte de Beaune AC for its limpid lightish jewel-ruby colour, insistent English-cherry nose and clingy yet elusive raspberry-and-cream delicate fruit; proper red burgundy, slick but wholesome; 14% alcohol. The price is mad but dictated, unfortunately, by a market insane for quality burgundy at every level.

FRANCE

RED WINES

ITALY

🍷 **10 Terre de Faiano Organic Primitivo 2022** £10.99
Perennial Puglian favourite billed as 'the first organic Primitivo made 100% by the appassimento method' is as soupily seductive as ever in this splendid 2022 vintage: dark chocolate in colour with a trace of cocoa savour amid the warm black berry fruits redolent of cinnamon, cloves and pepper, sweetly ripe but brisk at the finish; 13.5% alcohol. Stop press: a 1.5 litre (equal to two bottles) box suddenly appeared in 2024 at £19.99. I bought one (for £15 on promo) and can confirm the wine was just as good, especially at the equivalent of £7.50 a bottle.

🍷 **9 Venturina Freisa d'Asti 2022** £10.99
Ghastly magenta labelling ill serves this delightful Piedmont juice-bomb from freisa grapes (related to nebbiolo of Barolo renown), but it's a treat: Beaujolais-like bouncy raspberry style but with a good heft and firm tannins, brisk at the finish; 12.5% alcohol. Good summer red, it looks a bit pricey but at the £7.99 I paid, a proper bargain.

🍷 **8 Banfi Centine Toscana Rosso 2020** £12.99
Generic wine from Chiantishire is made with declassified fruit from the almighty American-owned Banfi estate at Montalcino, source of very grand brunello wines. I liked this sangiovese, cabernet and merlot blend, light-ish, chianti-like with oak heft and true to quality Tuscan style; 13.5% alcohol. Waitrose Cellar only.

RED WINES

♀ 10 Pazzia Primitivo di Manduria 2021 £12.99

The distinctive striped label makes this potent Puglia wine easy to pick out – which you should do at once. It's velvety in rich dark colour, intense in its opulent pruny-briar fruit and reassuring in its cushiony heft; 14% alcohol. It's regularly on promo at £9.99. Manduria is in the Salento, top spot for primitivo, and this wine makes a consoling substitute for Trulli Salice Salentino, a Waitrose wonder inexplicably dumped from the list last year.

♀ 8 Villa Cafaggio Chianti Classico 2021 £14.99

Unusually for a Chianti Classico, this is 100% sangiovese, organically produced, and it does have a certain purity about its opulent, dark sour cherry fruit; 13.5% alcohol. Better – richer and more rounded (some oak ageing) – than I remember from previous vintages and good value when discounted – as it often is – to £10.99 and also available in rather good magnum size.

♀ 9 ColleMassari Montecucco Rosso Riserva 2019 £15.99

I liked the look of this posh organic Tuscan number at my local store and fell for the offer at £10.99. It's a variation on Chianti, mostly sangiovese, from an obscure neighbouring DOC, Montecucco, on the coast, and has focused density of jewel-like colour and rich oak-enhanced fruit with trademark sangiovese edginess and brisk tannins; plush and poised and easily worth the shelf ticket let alone the mad promo price; 14.5% alcohol. It should age long and gracefully.

RED WINES

NEW ZEALAND

8 **Mount Difficulty Pinot Noir 2021** **£29.99**

Thirty quid for a wine rather like grand burgundy is arguably a bargain, but you'll need to be a fan of the Kiwi style exemplified in this intense and potent (14% alcohol) Central Otago pinot. I liked its silky focus but suggest keeping it a year or three.

PORTUGAL

9 **Cantina Segreti Castelão 2021** **£8.99**

Redcurrant juiciness gives piquancy to this generous pure-varietal of mysterious origin (Cantina Segreti means 'secret cellar'); very likeable oak-smoothed food matcher of proper Portuguese spicy-herby character; 13.5% alcohol.

9 **Waitrose Loved & Found Touriga Nacional 2021** **£8.99**

I've never been to the Algarve – the resort region of southernmost Portugal – and had assumed it was all golf courses rather than vineyards, but here's a lovely brambly-raspberry spin on the great grape of Port country (500km to the north) that's well up to par. Juicy but wholesomely substantial and plumped with oak contact, it's poised and elegantly weighted; 14% alcohol. Nice jampot-label presentation in Waitrose's nascent Loved & Found range from unexpected places.

ROMANIA

8 **Waitrose Blueprint Romanian Pinot Noir 2023** **£6.99**

Pale but not wan, an earthy summer-red-fruit pinot with good shape and finish; 13% alcohol. Much better than the dreary collective-farm Romanian plonk of yesteryear, and at a keen price.

RED WINES

SOUTH AFRICA

🍷 **8** **Fire Flower Shiraz 2023** £8.99

Unlike the cushiony style of Aussie shiraz this Cape variation on the familiar upfront-fruit theme is light in colour and quite firm in texture with spiky black berry fruit; 14% alcohol.

SPAIN

🍷 **10** **Heredad del Rey Monastrell Syrah 2020** £6.99

Gorgeous sinewy blueberry-blackberry lipsmacker from the sequestered DO of Yecla just south of Alicante is terrific in this vintage; 13.5% alcohol. Oak-matured and plushly silky it tastes way above the humble price (and I paid just over a fiver on promo); an extraordinary bargain in a cute retro package complete with smart screwcap.

🍷 **7** **Marques de Calatrava Reserva**
Tempranillo 2015 £8.99

Aged for 20 months in oak barrels' proclaims the label on this wire-caged, heraldically emblazoned La Mancha throwing wine, but I couldn't help liking its old-fashioned, slightly weedy style, the fruit valiantly tilting at the wood in what is after all a ten-year combat; 13% alcohol. I paid £6.99 on promo and it's pretty much what you can expect for this money.

🍷 **8** **Viña Arana Rioja Gran Reserva 2016** £36.99

The intense colour is browning discreetly and the aromas embrace a sort of gaminess alongside the silky-minty still-bright fruitiness and creaminess of long-oaking. Deluxe but not showy mature top-line Rioja for very special occasions; 14% alcohol.

PINK WINES

8 Isula Mea Syrah-Sciaccarellu Rosé 2023   £9.99

Very pale, very dry but pleasingly nuanced pink from Corsica under the fancifully named IGP Ile de Beauté; stands out from the Mediterranean crowd for its savoury evocations of the island's wildly aromatic maquis landscape; 12.5% alcohol. Or maybe I'm just imagining it.

8 Eminence de Bijou 2023   £14.99

It's from the Coteaux de Béziers in the Languedoc-Roussillon, a region to watch for distinctive wines right now, an elegantly packaged and copper-coloured pink of sleek raspberry-rose-petal aroma and fruit, very poised and clear, refreshing and citrus-tangy at the edge; 12.5% alcohol. Premium pink that for once just about merits the price point.

8 Minuty Rosé 2023   £19.99

You'd have to be a dedicated pinkster to pay twenty quid for a rosé, but if there's one I've tasted this year I guess this posh Provence item is it. Alluring onion-skin colour, bright seaside-fresh aromas of redcurrant and alpine strawberry, corresponding fruit with palpable structure as well as vividness and zing, genuinely refreshing and stimulating; 13% alcohol.

8 Loved & Found Organic Susumaniello Rosato 2023   £7.99

Pale, soft but not without some gentle red-summer-berry-fruit juiciness, a Puglian authentic pink with balance and brightness, quite dry; 12.5% alcohol.

8 Loved & Found Organic Aglianico Rosato 2023 £8.99

Properly made Puglia wine entirely from black-skinned aglianico grapes macerated on their skins for eight hours to create the pleasing delicate shell-pink colour and imparting some real fruit character too. Good, juicy, clear, very dry refresher, and thoroughly Italian; 12.5% alcohol.

WHITE WINES

AUSTRALIA

8 **Elephant in the Room Voluminous Viognier 2023** £10.99
Expansive ripe dry wine from Victoria state with the expected viognier exotic fruit style and plenty of interest above and beyond the attention-demanding name, for which I can find no explanation; 14.5% alcohol.

AUSTRIA

9 **Blueprint Grüner Veltliner 2023** £8.99
Produced for Waitrose by celebrated Niederösterreich (prime vineyard region) winemaker Markus Huber, a prickly-fresh, herbaceous and finely balanced own-label of real quality – and value; 12.5% alcohol.

8 **Waitrose Loved & Found Gelber Muskateller 2023** £8.99
It's a dry muscat, really, with just a suggestion of nectar sweetness to follow up the floral aroma and lively freshness; 12% alcohol. Good to see such a delicate aperitif wine among the new Loved & Found range.

FRANCE

8 **Le Sablou Sauvignon Blanc 2022** £8.99
From the Bordeaux satellite of Bergerac, a better wine than I expected (always had doubts about Bergerac) it's all-sauvignon and generously coloured and ripe; lively grassy and quite lush; 13% alcohol.

10 **La Perrière Touraine Sauvignon Blanc 2023** £9.99
This one jumped out of the crowd of sauvignons from everywhere that I've tasted this year. Touraine is a regional appellation, after its historic capital of Tours, for wines from the middle section of the Loire Valley and I believe it's a name to watch. This one has delightfully sherbetty zing to its grassy green fruit, sunny ripeness and poised purity, really special; 13% alcohol.

WHITE WINES

8 **Laurent Miquel Vendanges Nocturnes Viognier 2023** £9.99

Artfully made Languedoc dry wine from 100% viognier grapes harvested at night for fruit coolness; ripe stone-fruit flavours including apricot and nectarine but bright freshness and zest in equal measure; 13% alcohol.

9 **Cave de Turckheim Gewürztraminer 2022** £11.49

Turckheim is one of Alsace's leading co-operative wine producers and seems to supply just about every British supermarket with basic Gewürztraminer, the most exotic of the region's highly distinctive wines. This one's particularly good in this vintage: lavish colour, classic lychee and rose petal nose, plenty of spicy weight to the luxuriant fruit and not too sweet; 13% alcohol.

9 **Wolfberger Pinot Blanc 2020** £11.49

A rare treat – Alsace's least-celebrated grape the pinot blanc in its ideal unblended glory delivers herbaceous green-fruit lushness with a brassica crispness all its own; 12.5% alcohol. It's very dry but craftily rich with a suggestion of blanched-almond creaminess. Versatile food matcher. Wolfberger is the brand name of the excellent wine co-operative of the beautiful Alsace town of Eguisheim.

8 **Pouilly-Fumé Domaine Masson-Blondelet 2023** £16.99

Prestige Loire Valley pure sauvignon; plush in colour, crisply green and mineral on the nose and full of slaking river-pebble freshness; 13% alcohol.

WHITE WINES

FRANCE

🍷 8 **Saint-Aubin 1er Cru Domaine
Gérard Thomas 2022** £36.99

Saint-Aubin in the Côte de Beaune makes some of the more affordable burgundies and this one, pure chardonnay barrel fermented to give a creamy style to the opulent yet steely fruit, is certainly delicious and possibly worth the price; 13% alcohol.

GERMANY

🍷 8 **Blueprint Dry German Riesling 2023** £8.49

Notable pale gold colour and keen crisp-apple'n'lime aroma to this racy house moselle, fresh, long and indeed dry; 12% alcohol.

GREECE

🍷 8 **Zacharias Assyrtiko 2023** £12.99

Maybe the supermarkets should look a bit beyond the ubiquitous assyrtiko grape for their Greek white wines, but this one does have its own charms. From Nemea in the Peloponnese it's like a particularly succulent sauvignon blanc, emerald in glitter, very fresh with white orchard fruit and satisfying in its mouthfilling bloom, ripe but balanced with a citrus twang; 13% alcohol.

ITALY

🍷 8 **Il Grifone d'Oro Soave Classico 2023** £8.99

Proper Soave of good gold colour with green flashes, a bright cabbagey-grassy aroma and frankly assertive crisp white fruits harbouring sweet almond richness; good food matcher and very fresh; 12.5% alcohol.

WHITE WINES

10 Tre Fiori Greco di Tufo 2022 £11.99

The best greco I've tasted in a long while. Plush colour, zingy apple-lemon nose, bracing but seductive entry flowing into a basket of fresh fruit flavours with ideal citrus twang. And it tastes convincingly as it should, from the revived grape variety first planted by ancient Greek settlers here in the lush, volcanic Campania, three thousand years ago. A grand aperitif, and ideal match for creamy pasta as well as fishy dishes; 13% alcohol.

8 Piccozza Pinot Bianco 2023 £12.99

From the sub-Alpine Alto Adige a copiously coloured aromatic pinot blanc familiar from the herbaceous-appley Alsace style but with its own minerality and crispness; 13.5% alcohol.

10 Blueprint Vinho Verde 2023 £6.99

Perfect! Crisp green-apple fruit has a positive prickle of freshness in this ideally made VV. The residual sugar, retained so this dry wine isn't too 'green' for export markets is here unusually well judged, so you get true fruit instead of dull sweetness. Just 10.5% alcohol and a very keen price.

9 Waitrose Loved & Found Cerceal 2023 £8.99

Cerceal is the grape, here grown in the Dâo region to make this outstanding lemon-gold and agreeably hefty dry wine reminiscent of fino sherry in weight with ripe tropical notes amid the clear white fruits; 12.5% alcohol. Nice match for sardines, mackerel and other oily fish.

WHITE WINES

8 **A.A. Badenhorst The Curator White Blend 2023** **£9.99**
Fruit-salad blend of half chenin blanc and the rest mainly
chardonnay and viognier has the signature nectar-citrus
paradox of that noble grape the chenin, delivering a dry wine
of delightful savour and freshness; 13% alcohol.

8 **Boschendal Sommelier Selection**
Chardonnay 2022 **£11.99**
Wholesome oaked pure chardonnay with a friendly lick of
toffee amid the poised red-apple and white-peach fruit; 13.5%
alcohol.

8 **CVNE Bodegas La Val Albariño 2023** **£16.99**
Rioja outfit CVNE's Rias Baixas vineyards do well with this
big-colour and big-flavour leesy and sea-breezy albariño in the
best local tradition: ripe white grassy fruit with limey tang and
lasting savours; 12.5% alcohol.

8 **The Federalist Chardonnay 2022** **£19.99**
Grand Californian wine in the white burgundy manner – a
third of the blend has been aged in new oak casks – is lavish but
artfully contrived for minerality and brisk citrus twang; classy
and fun, and by burgundy standards, modestly priced; 14.5%
alcohol. Waitrose Cellar only.

FORTIFIED WINES

8 **Blueprint Tawny Port** **£9.49**
New to me in the expanding Blueprint own-label range a likeable
and by no means oversweet 'tawny' port so-called because it's
been cask-aged rather than bottle-aged and is entirely ruby in
colour, a nicely integrated wine to enjoy chilled as an aperitif
(the way the Portuguese do) at a pretty good price, especially
the £7-ish I paid on promo; 19% alcohol.

SOUTH AFRICA

SPAIN

USA

PORTUGAL

FORTIFIED WINES

🍷 10 Graham's 10-Year-Old Tawny Port £23.49

Graham's is the best 10-year-old tawny port on the market by a country mile but not, sadly, the cheapest. Save up for this but also look out for discounts including Waitrose's occasional 25% off all wines, which sometimes includes fortified. Not yet tawny in colour but a lovely slightly orange ruby, the Graham's is pure silk with a heady nose of creamy nuts, ripe figs, Christmas in redolent metaphor, and a shock of rich, fiery, honeyed and sharpening fruit; perfect balance; 20% alcohol.

🍷 8 Pedro's Almacenista Selection Amontillado
Medium Dry Sherry £11.49

From Waitrose's lately launched Pedro's range of almacenista (small-scale, often high-quality producer) sherries, a heady, luxuriant amber-gold wine of sweet-nut savour that's also delicate, balanced and briskly *rancio*; 19% alcohol. Don't be put off by the retro labelling – featuring the poster for the 1955 Jerez harvest festival – and unexpected screwcap. Served chilled in a proper wine glass, this is a world-class aperitif.

SPARKLING WINES

🍷 10 Chapel Down Brut NV £28.99

The quality of English sparkling wine has finally caught up with the price. Objectively, I assert that this one is as good as big-brand champagne costing the same or more. Made in Kent from chardonnay, pinots meunier and noir (the stock varieties for champagne) and a little pinot blanc harvested locally and in Sussex, Essex and Dorset and made by precisely the same elaborate method as champagne, it has busy tiny-bubble mousse, warmly yeasty textbook orchard-citrus-hothouse fruits, crispness and ebullience and 12% alcohol. The case is made. Bravo Chapel Down.

SPARKLING WINES

ENGLAND

Y 9 **Hattingley Valley Classic Reserve NV** £33.99
Richly coloured Hampshire sparkler's variation on the burgeoning English-fizz theme is that a fifth of the must from the chardonnay/pinot fruit was fermented in old white-burgundy casks. The style of the finished wine is generously ripe and lush, the opulent fruit carried along on a wave of creamy fizz, full and perfectly crisp; 12% alcohol.

FRANCE

Y 9 **Crémant de Bourgogne Brut Blanc de Blancs** £15.99
Consistent all-chardonnay vigorous sparkler from the excellent Cave de Lugny in the Mâconnais has a creaminess of red-apple fruitiness as well as the kind of 'creaming' mousse that is rightly reflected in rising sales of crémant wines from French regions including not just Burgundy, but Alsace, the Jura and Loire. This one is briskly fresh but full of interest into the bargain – which it frequently is on discount to £11.99; 11.5% alcohol.

Y 8 **Le Mesnil Blanc de Blancs Grand**
Cru Champagne Brut NV £39.99
Chi-chi all-chardonnay champagne has soft but persistent mousse, mellow brioche richness (five years' bottle ageing after disgorgement) and elegant balance of fruit and acidity, lavish but decidely 'brut'; 12.5% alcohol. Safe bet for grand celebrations.

ITALY

Y 8 **Loved & Found Ribolla Gialla Spumante** £8.99
Wildly fizzy and brimming with juicy orchard fruit, a crisp and balanced refresher from Friuli in northeast Italy, unrelated to prosecco and certainly more interesting; 11% alcohol. Scores for value too.

SPARKLING WINES

🍷 8 Bersano Monteolivo Moscato d'Asti 2023   £9.99
Honeyed Piedmont fizz from sweet muscat grapes, artfully balanced between richness and refreshingness and just 5.5% alcohol. Party aperitif and natural partner for sticky-bun occasions. Waitrose Cellar only.

🍷 8 Valdo Aquarius Rosé Brut NV   £12.99
Tank-method petal-pink fizz from Veneto has a strawberry note to the apple-pear fruit in the soft but lively mousse, a rather charmingly fresh alternative to prosecco; 11% alcohol.

Enjoying it

Drink or keep?

Wines from supermarkets should be ready to drink as soon as you get them home. Expensive reds of recent vintage, for example from Bordeaux or the Rhône, sold as seasonal specials, might benefit from a few years' 'cellaring'. If in doubt, look up your purchase on a web vintage chart to check.

Some wines certainly need drinking sooner than others. Dry whites and rosés won't improve with time. Good-quality red wines will happily endure, even improve, for years if they're kept at a constant moderate temperature, preferably away from bright light, and on their sides so corks don't dry out. Supermarkets like to advise us on back labels of red wines to consume the product within a year or two. Pay no attention.

Champagne, including supermarket own-label brands, almost invariably improves with keeping. Evolving at rest is what champagne is all about. Continue the process at home. I like to wait for price promotions, buy in bulk and hoard the booty in smug certainty of a bargain that's also an improving asset. None of this applies to any other kind of sparkling wine – especially prosecco.

Of more immediate urgency is the matter of keeping wine in good condition once you've opened it. Recorked leftovers should last a day, but after that the wine will oxidise, turning stale and sour. There is a variety of wine-saving stopper devices, but I have yet to find one that works. My preferred method is to decant leftovers into a smaller bottle with a pull-cork or screwcap. Top it right up.

Early opening

Is there any point in uncorking a wine in advance to allow it to 'breathe'? Absolutely none. The stale air trapped between the top of the wine and the bottom of the cork (or screwcap) disperses at once and the 1cm circle of liquid exposed will have a negligible response to the atmosphere. Decanting the wine will certainly make a difference, but whether it's a beneficial difference is a matter for conjecture – unless you're decanting to get the wine off its lees or sediment.

Beware trying to warm up an icy bottle of red. If you put it close to a heat source, take the cork out first. As the wine warms, even mildly, it gives off gas that will spoil the flavour if it cannot escape.

Chill factor

White wine, rosé and sparkling wines all need to be cold. It's the law. The degree of chill is a personal choice but icy temperatures can mask the flavours of good wines. Bad wines, on the other hand, might benefit from overchilling. The anaesthetic effect removes the sense of taste.

Red wines can respond well to mild chilling. Beaujolais and stalky reds of the Loire such as Chinon and Saumur are brighter when cool, as is Bardolino from Verona and lighter Pinot Noir from everywhere.

Is it off?

Once there was a plague of 'corked' wine. It's over. Wine bottlers have eliminated most of the causes. Principal among them was TCA or trichloroanisole 123, an infection of the raw material from which corks are made, namely the bark of cork oak trees. New technology developed by firms such as Portuguese cork giant Amorim has finally made all cork taint-free.

TCA spawned an alternative-closure industry that has prospered mightily through the supply of polymer stoppers and screwcaps. The polymer products, although unnecessary now that corks are so reliable, persist. They're pointless: awkward to extract and to reinsert, and allegedly less environmentally friendly than natural corks.

Screwcaps persist too, but they have their merits. They obviate the corkscrew and can be replaced on the bottle. They are recyclable. Keep them on the bottles you take to the bottle bank.

Some closures will, of course, occasionally fail due to material faults or malfunctions in bottling that allow air into the bottle. The dull, sour effects on wine of oxidation are obvious, and you should return any offending bottle to the supplier for a replacement or refund. Supermarkets in my experience are pretty good about this.

Wines that are bad because they are poorly made are a bit more complicated. You might just hate it because it's not to your taste – too sweet or too dry, too dense or too light – in which case, bad luck. But if it has classic (though now rare) faults such as mustiness, a vinegar taint (volatile acidity or acetate), cloudiness or a suspension of particles, don't drink it. Recork it and take it back to the supplier.

Glass action

There is something like a consensus in the wine world about the right kind of drinking glass. It should consist of a clear, tulip-shaped bowl on a comfortably long stem. You hold the glass by the stem so you can admire the colour of the wine and keep the bowl free of fingermarks. The bowl is big enough to hold a sensible quantity of wine at about half full. Good wine glasses have a fine bevelled surface at the rim of the bowl. Cheap glasses have a rolled rim that catches your lip and, I believe, materially diminishes the enjoyment of the wine.

Good wine glasses deserve care. Don't put them in the dishwasher. Over time, they'll craze. To maintain the crystal clarity of glasses wash them in hot soapy water, rinse clean with hot water and dry immediately with a glass cloth kept exclusively for this purpose. Sounds a bit nerdy maybe, but it can make all the difference.

What to eat with it?

When tasting a hundred or more wines one after the other and trying to make lucid notes on each of them, the mind can crave diversion. Besides describing the appearance, aroma and taste, as I'm supposed to do, I often muse on what sort of food the wine might suit.

Some of these whimsical observations make it into the finished reports for this book. Like all the rest of it, they are my own subjective opinion, but maybe they help set the wines in some sort of context.

Conventions such as white wine with fish and red with meat might be antiquated, but they can still inhibit choice. If you only like white wine must you abstain on carnivorous occasions – or go veggie? Obviously not. Much better to give detailed thought to the possibilities, and go in for plenty of experimentation.

Ripe whites from grapes such as Chardonnay can match all white meats, cured meats and barbecued meats, and most saucy meat dishes too. With bloody chunks of red meat, exotic whites from the Rhône Valley or Alsace or oaky Rioja Blanco all come immediately to mind.

As for those who prefer red wine at all times, there are few fish dishes that spurn everything red. Maybe a crab salad or a grilled Dover sole. But as soon as you add sauce, red's back on the menu. Again, the answer is to experiment.

Some foods do present particular difficulties. Nibbles such as salty peanuts or vinegary olives will clash with most table wines. So buy some proper dry sherry, chill it down and thrill to the world's best aperitif. Fino, manzanilla and amontillado sherries of real quality now feature in all the best supermarkets – some under own labels.

Eggs are supposed to be inimical to wine. Boiled, fried or poached certainly. But an omelette with a glass of wine, of any colour, is surely a match. Salads, especially those with fruit or tomatoes, get the thumbs-down, but I think it's the dressing. Forgo the vinegar, and salad opens up a vinous vista.

Cheese is a conundrum. Red wine goes with cheese, right? But soft cheeses, particularly goat's, can make red wines taste awfully tinny. You're much better off with an exotic and ripe white wine. Sweet white wines make a famously savoury match with blue cheeses. A better match, I believe, than with their conventional companions, puddings. Hard cheeses such as Cheddar may be fine with some red wines, but even better with a glass of Port.

Wine with curry? Now that incendiary dishes are entirely integrated into the national diet, I suppose this is, uh, a burning question. Big, ripe reds such as Australian Shiraz can stand up to Indian heat, and Argentine Malbec seems appropriate for chilli dishes. Chinese cuisine likes aromatic white wines such as Alsace (or New Zealand) Gewürztraminer, and salsa dishes call for zingy dry whites such as Sauvignon Blanc.

But everyone to their own taste. If there's one universal convention in food and wine matching it must surely be to suit yourself.

—A Wine Vocabulary—

A brief guide to the use of language across the wine world – on labels, in literature and among the listings in this book

A

AC/AOC – *See* Appellation d'Origine Contrôlée.

acidity – Natural acids in grape juice are harnessed by the winemaker to produce clean, crisp flavours. Excess acidity creates rawness or greenness; shortage is indicated by wateriness.

aftertaste – The flavour that lingers in the mouth after swallowing or spitting the wine.

Aglianico – Black grape variety of southern Italy. Vines originally planted by ancient Greek settlers from 600BC in the arid volcanic landscapes of Basilicata and Cilento produce distinctive dark and earthy reds.

Agriculture biologique – On French wine labels, an indication that the wine has been made by organic methods.

Albariño – White grape variety of Spain that makes intriguingly perfumed fresh and tangy dry wines, especially in esteemed Atlantic-facing Rias Baixas region.

alcohol – The alcohol levels in wines are expressed in terms of alcohol by volume ('abv'), that is, the percentage of the volume of the wine that is common, or ethyl, alcohol. A typical wine at 12 per cent abv is thus 12 parts alcohol and, in effect, 88 parts fruit juice. Alcohol is viewed by some health professionals as a poison, but there is actuarial evidence that total abstainers live shorter lives than moderate consumers. The UK Department of Health declares there is no safe level of alcohol consumption, and advises that drinkers should not exceed a weekly number of 'units' of alcohol. A unit is 10ml of pure alcohol, the quantity contained in about half a 175ml glass of wine with 12 per cent alcohol. From 1995, the advisory limit on weekly units was 28 for men and 21 for women. This was reduced in 2016 to 14 for men and women alike.

Alentejo – Wine region of southern Portugal (immediately north of the Algarve), with a fast-improving reputation, especially for sappy, keen reds from local grape varieties including Aragones, Castelão and Trincadeira.

Almansa – DO winemaking region of Spain inland from Alicante, making inexpensive red wines.

Alsace – France's easternmost wine-producing region lies between the Vosges Mountains and the River Rhine, with Germany beyond. These conditions make for the production of some of the world's most delicious and fascinating white wines, always sold under the name of their constituent grapes. Pinot Blanc is the most affordable – and is well worth looking out for. The 'noble' grape varieties of the region are Gewürztraminer, Muscat, Riesling and Pinot Gris and they are always made on a single-variety basis. The richest, most exotic wines are those from individual *grand cru* vineyards, which are named on the label. Some *vendange tardive* (late harvest) wines are made, and tend to be expensive. All the wines are sold in tall, slim green bottles known as flûtes that closely resemble those of the Mosel. The names of producers as well as grape varieties are often German too, so it is widely assumed that Alsace wines are German in style, if not in nationality. But this is not the case in either particular. Alsace wines are dry and quite unique in character – and definitely French.

amarone – Style of red wine made in Valpolicella, Italy. Specially selected grapes are held back from the harvest and stored for several months to dry them out. They are then pressed and fermented into a highly concentrated speciality dry wine. Amarone means 'bitter', describing the dry style of the flavour.

AP/AOP – *See* Appellation d'Origine Protégée.

aperitif – If a wine is thus described, I believe it will give as much pleasure before a meal as with one. Crisp, low-alcohol German wines and other delicately flavoured whites (including many dry Italians) are examples.

appassimento – Italian technique of drying out new-picked grapes to concentrate the sugars. Varying proportions of appassimento fruit are added to the fermentation of speciality wines such as amarone and ripasso.

Appellation d'Origine Contrôlée – Commonly abbreviated to AC or AOC, this is the system under which top-quality wines have been defined in France since 1935. About a third of the country's vast annual output qualifies across about 500 AC (or AOP – see Appellation d'Origine Protégée) zones. The declaration of an AC on the label signifies that the wine meets standards concerning location of vineyards and wineries, grape varieties and limits on harvest per hectare, methods of cultivation and vinification, and alcohol content. Wines are inspected and tasted by state-appointed committees.

Appellation d'Origine Protégée (AOP) – Under European Union rule changes, the AOC system is gradually transforming into AOP. In effect, it means little more than the exchange of 'controlled' with 'protected' on labels. One quirk of the rules is that makers of AOP wines will be able to name the constituent grape variety or varieties on their labels, if they so wish.

Apulia – Anglicised name for Puglia, Italy.

Aragones – Synonym in Portugal, especially in the Alentejo region, for the Tempranillo grape variety of Spain.

Ardèche – Region of southern France to the west of the Rhône river, home to a good IGP zone including the Coteaux de l'Ardèche. Decent-value reds from Syrah and Cabernet Sauvignon grapes, and less interesting dry whites.

Arneis – White grape variety of Piedmont, north-west Italy. Makes dry whites with a certain almondy richness at often-inflated prices.

Assyrtiko – White grape variety of Greece now commonly named on dry white wines, sometimes of great quality, from the mainland and islands.

Asti – Town and major winemaking centre in Piedmont, Italy. The sparkling (spumante) wines made from Moscato grapes are inexpensive and sweet with a modest 5 to 7 per cent alcohol. Vivid red wine Barbera d'Asti also produced.

attack – In wine-tasting, the first impression made by the wine in the mouth.

Auslese – German wine-quality designation. *See* QmP.

B

Baga – Black grape variety indigenous to Portugal. Makes famously concentrated, juicy reds of deep colour from the grapes' particularly thick skins. Look out for this name, now quite frequently quoted as the varietal on Portuguese wine labels.

balance – A big word in the vocabulary of wine tasting. Respectable wine must get two key things right: lots of fruitiness from the sweet grape juice, and plenty of acidity so the sweetness is 'balanced' with the crispness familiar in good dry whites and the dryness that marks out good reds. Some wines are noticeably 'well balanced' in that they have memorable fruitiness and the clean, satisfying 'finish' (last flavour in the mouth) that ideal acidity imparts.

Barbera – Black grape variety originally of Piedmont in Italy. Most commonly seen as Barbera d'Asti, the vigorously fruity red wine made around Asti – once better known for sweet sparkling Asti Spumante. Barbera grapes are now cultivated in South America, producing less-interesting wine than at home in Italy.

Bardolino – Once fashionable, light red wine DOC of Veneto, north-west Italy. Bardolino is made principally from Corvina Veronese grapes plus Rondinella, Molinara and Negrara. Best wines are supposed to be those labelled Bardolino Superiore, a DOCG created in 2002. This classification closely specifies the permissible grape varieties and sets the alcohol level at a minimum of 12 per cent.

Barossa Valley – Famed vineyard region north of Adelaide, Australia, produces hearty reds principally from Shiraz, Cabernet Sauvignon and Grenache grapes, plus plenty of lush white wine from Chardonnay. Also known for limey, long-lived, mineral dry whites from Riesling grapes.

barrique – Barrel in French. *En barrique* on a wine label signifies the wine has been matured in casks rather than tanks.

Beaujolais – Unique red wines from the southern reaches of Burgundy, France, are made from Gamay grapes. Beaujolais nouveau, now unfashionable, provides a friendly introduction to the bouncy, red-fruit style of the wine, but for the authentic experience, go for Beaujolais Villages, from the region's better, northern vineyards. There are ten AC zones within this northern sector making wines under their own names. Known as the *crus*, these are Brouilly, Chénas, Chiroubles, Côte de Brouilly, Fleurie, Juliénas, Morgon, Moulin à Vent, Regnié and St Amour. Prices are higher than those for Beaujolais Villages, but not always justifiably so.

Beaumes de Venise – Village near Châteauneuf du Pape in France's Rhône valley, famous for sweet and alcoholic wine from Muscat grapes. Delicious, grapey wines. A small number of growers also make strong (sometimes rather tough) red wines under the village name.

Beaune – One of the two centres (the other is Nuits St Georges) of the Côte d'Or, the winemaking heart of Burgundy in France. Three of the region's humbler appellations take the name of the town: Côtes de Beaune, Côtes de Beaune Villages and Hautes Côtes de Beaune.

berry fruit – Some red wines deliver a burst of flavour in the mouth that corresponds to biting into a newly picked berry – strawberry, blackberry, etc. So a wine described as having berry fruit (by this writer, anyway) has freshness, liveliness and immediate appeal.

bianco – White wine, Italy.

Bical – White grape variety principally of Dão region of northern Portugal. Not usually identified on labels, because most of it goes into inexpensive sparkling wines. Can make still wines of very refreshing crispness.

biodynamics – A cultivation method taking the organic approach several steps further. Biodynamic winemakers plant and tend their vineyards according to a date and time calendar 'in harmony' with the movements of the planets. Some of France's best-known wine estates subscribe, and many more are going that way. It might all sound bonkers, but it's salutary to learn that biodynamics is based on principles first described by the eminent Austrian educationist Rudolph Steiner.

bite – In wine-tasting, the impression on the palate of a wine with plenty of acidity and, often, tannin.

blanc – White wine, France.

blanc de blancs – White wine from white grapes, France. May seem to be stating the obvious, but some white wines (e.g. champagne) are made, partially or entirely, from black grapes.

blanc de noirs – White wine from black grapes, France. Usually sparkling (especially champagne) made from black Pinot Meunier and Pinot Noir grapes, with no Chardonnay or other white varieties.

blanco – White wine, Spain and Portugal.

Blauer Zweigelt – Black grape variety of Austria, making a large proportion of the country's red wines, some of excellent quality.

Bobal – Black grape variety mostly of south-eastern Spain. Thick skin is good for colour and juice contributes acidity to blends.

bodega – In Spain, a wine producer or wine shop.

Bonarda – Black grape variety of northern Italy. Now more widely planted in Argentina, where it makes some well-regarded red wines.

botrytis – Full name, *botrytis cinerea*, is that of a beneficent fungus that can attack ripe grape bunches late in the season, shrivelling the berries to a gruesome-looking mess, which yields concentrated juice of prized sweetness. Cheerfully known as 'noble rot', this fungus is actively encouraged by winemakers in regions as diverse as Sauternes (in Bordeaux), Monbazillac (in Bergerac), the Rhine and Mosel valleys, Hungary's Tokaji region and South Australia to make ambrosial dessert wines.

bouncy – The feel in the mouth of a red wine with young, juicy fruitiness. Good Beaujolais is bouncy, as are many north-west-Italian wines from Barbera and Dolcetto grapes.

Bourgogne Grand Ordinaire – Former AC of Burgundy, France. *See* Coteaux Bourguignons.

Bourgueil – Appellation of Loire Valley, France. Long-lived red wines from Cabernet Franc grapes.

briary – In wine tasting, associated with the flavours of fruit from prickly bushes such as blackberries.

brûlé – Pleasant burnt-toffee taste or smell, as in crème brûlée.

brut – Driest style of sparkling wine. Originally French, for very dry champagnes specially developed for the British market, but now used for sparkling wines from all round the world.

Buzet – Little-seen AC of south-west France overshadowed by Bordeaux but producing some characterful ripe reds.

C

Cabardès – AC for red and rosé wines from area north of Carcassonne, Aude, France. Principally Cabernet Sauvignon and Merlot grapes.

Cabernet Franc – Black grape variety originally of France. It makes the light-bodied and keenly edged red wines of the Loire Valley – such as Chinon and Saumur. And it is much grown in Bordeaux, especially in the appellation of St Emilion. Also now planted in Argentina, Australia and North America. Wines, especially in the Loire, are characterised by a leafy, sappy style and bold fruitiness. Most are best enjoyed young.

Cabernet Sauvignon – Black (or, rather, blue) grape variety now grown in virtually every wine-producing nation. When perfectly ripened, the grapes are smaller than many other varieties and have particularly thick skins.

This means that when pressed, Cabernet grapes have a high proportion of skin to juice – and that makes for wine with lots of colour and tannin. In Bordeaux, the grape's traditional home, the grandest Cabernet-based wines have always been known as *vins de garde* (wines to keep) because they take years, even decades, to evolve as the effect of all that skin extraction preserves the fruit all the way to magnificent maturity. But in today's impatient world, these grapes are exploited in modern winemaking techniques to produce the sublime flavours of mature Cabernet without having to hang around for lengthy periods awaiting maturation. While there's nothing like a fine, ten-year-old claret (and few quite as expensive), there are many excellent Cabernets from around the world that amply illustrate this grape's characteristics. Classic smells and flavours include blackcurrants, cedar wood, chocolate, tobacco – even violets.

Cahors – An AC of the Lot Valley in south-west France once famous for 'black wine'. This was a curious concoction of straightforward wine mixed with a soupy must, made by boiling up new-pressed juice to concentrate it (through evaporation) before fermentation. The myth is still perpetuated that Cahors wine continues to be made in this way, but production on this basis actually ceased 150 years ago. Cahors today is no stronger, or blacker, than the wines of neighbouring appellations. Principal grape variety is Malbec, known locally as Cot.

Cairanne – Village of the appellation collectively known as the Côtes du Rhône in southern France. Cairanne is one of several villages entitled to put their name on the labels of wines made within their AC boundary, and appearance of this name is quite reliably an indicator of quality.

Calatayud – DO (quality wine zone) near Zaragoza in the Aragon region of northern Spain where they're making some astonishingly good wines at bargain prices, mainly reds from Garnacha and Tempranillo grapes. These are the varieties that go into the polished and oaky wines of Rioja, but in Calatayud, the wines are dark, dense and decidedly different.

Cannonau – Black grape native to Sardinia by name, but in fact the same variety as the ubiquitous Grenache of France (and Garnacha of Spain).

cantina sociale – *See* co-op.

Carignan – Black grape variety of Mediterranean France. It is rarely identified on labels, but is a major constituent of wines from the southern Rhône and Languedoc-Roussillon regions. Known as Carignano in Italy and Cariñena in Spain.

Cariñena – A region of north-east Spain, south of Navarra, known for substantial reds, as well as the Spanish name for the Carignan grape (*qv*).

Carmenère – Black grape variety once widely grown in Bordeaux but abandoned due to cultivation problems. Lately revived in South America where it is producing fine wines, sometimes with echoes of Bordeaux.

cassis – As a tasting note, signifies a wine that has a noticeable blackcurrant-concentrate flavour or smell. Much associated with the Cabernet Sauvignon grape.

Castelao – Portuguese black grape variety. Same as Periquita.

Catarratto – White grape variety of Sicily. In skilled hands it can make anything from keen, green-fruit dry whites to lush, oaked super-ripe styles. Also used for Marsala.

cat's pee – In tasting notes, a jocular reference to the smell of a certain style of Sauvignon Blanc wine.

cava – The sparkling wine of Spain. Most originates in Catalonia, but the Denominación de Origen (DO) guarantee of authenticity is open to producers in many regions of the country. Much cava is very reasonably priced even though it is made by the same method as champagne – second fermentation in bottle, known in Spain as the *método clásico*.

CdR – Côtes du Rhône. My own shorthand.

cépage – Grape variety, French. 'Cépage Merlot' on a label simply means the wine is made largely or exclusively from Merlot grapes.

Chablis – Northernmost AC of France's Burgundy region. Its dry white wines from Chardonnay grapes are known for their fresh and steely style, but the best wines also age very gracefully into complex classics.

Chambourcin – Sounds like a cream cheese but it's a relatively modern (1963) French hybrid black grape that makes some good non-appellation lightweight-but-concentrated reds in the Loire Valley and now some heftier versions in Australia.

champagne – The sparkling wine of the strictly defined Champagne region of France, made by the equally strictly defined champagne method.

Chardonnay – Possibly the world's most popular grape variety. Said to originate from the village of Chardonnay in the Mâconnais region of southern Burgundy, the vine is now planted in every wine-producing nation. Wines are commonly characterised by generous colour and sweet-apple smell, but styles range from lean and sharp to opulently rich. Australia started the craze for oaked Chardonnay, the gold-coloured, super-ripe, buttery 'upfront' wines that are a caricature of lavish and outrageously expensive burgundies such as Meursault and Puligny-Montrachet. Rich to the point of egginess, these Aussie pretenders are now giving way to a sleeker, more minerally style with much less oak presence – if any at all. California and Chile, New Zealand and South Africa are competing hard to imitate the Burgundian style, and Australia's success in doing so.

Châteauneuf du Pape – Famed appellation centred on a picturesque village of the southern Rhône valley in France where in the 1320s French Pope Clement V had a splendid new château built for himself as a summer retreat amidst his vineyards. The red wines of the AC, which can be made from 13 different grape varieties but principally Grenache, Syrah and Mourvèdre, are regarded as the best of the southern Rhône and have become rather expensive – but they can be sensationally good. Expensive white wines are also made.

Chenin Blanc – White grape variety of the Loire Valley, France. Now also grown farther afield, especially in South Africa. Makes dry, soft white wines and also rich, sweet styles.

cherry – In wine tasting, either a pale red colour or, more commonly, a smell or flavour akin to the sun-warmed, bursting sweet ripeness of cherries. Many Italian wines, from lightweights such as Bardolino and Valpolicella to serious Chianti, have this character. 'Black cherry' as a description is often used of Merlot wines – meaning they are sweet but have a firmness of mouthfeel associated with the thicker skins of black cherries.

Cinsault – Black grape variety of southern France, where it is invariably blended with others in wines of all qualities from country reds to pricy appellations such as Châteauneuf du Pape. Also much planted in South Africa. The effect in wine is to add keen aromas (sometimes compared with turpentine) and softness to the blend. The name is often spelt Cinsaut.

Clape, La – A small *cru* (defined quality-vineyard area) within the Coteaux du Languedoc where the growers make some seriously delicious red wines, mainly from Carignan, Grenache and Syrah grapes. A name worth looking out for on labels from the region.

claret – The red wine of Bordeaux, France. Old British nickname from Latin *clarus*, meaning 'clear', recalling a time when the red wines of the region were much lighter in colour than they are now.

clarete – On Spanish labels indicates a pale-coloured red wine. Tinto signifies a deeper hue.

classed growth – English translation of French *cru classé* describes a group of 60 individual wine estates in the Médoc district of Bordeaux, which in 1855 were granted this new status on the basis that their wines were the most expensive of the day. The classification was a promotional wheeze to attract attention to the Bordeaux stand at that year's Great Exhibition in Paris. Amazingly, all of the wines concerned are still in production and most still occupy more or less their original places in the pecking order price-wise. The league was divided up into five divisions from *Premier Grand Cru Classé* (just four wines originally, with one promoted in 1971 – the only change ever made to the classification) to *Cinquième Grand Cru Classé*. Other regions of Bordeaux, notably Graves and St Emilion, have since imitated Médoc and introduced their own rankings of *cru classé* estates.

classic – An overused term in every respect – wine descriptions being no exception. In this book, the word is used to describe a very good wine of its type. So, a 'classic' Cabernet Sauvignon is one that is recognisably and admirably characteristic of that grape.

Classico – Under Italy's wine laws, this word appended to the name of a DOC or DOCG zone has an important significance. The classico wines of the region can only be made from vineyards lying in the best-rated areas, and wines thus labelled (e.g. Chianti Classico, Soave Classico, Valpolicella Classico) can be reliably counted on to be a cut above the rest.

Colombard – White grape variety of southern France. Once employed almost entirely for making the wine that is distilled for armagnac and cognac brandies, but lately restored to varietal prominence in the Côtes de Gascogne where high-tech wineries turn it into a fresh and crisp, if unchallenging, dry wine at a budget price. But beware, cheap Colombard (especially from South Africa) can still be very dull.

Conca de Barbera – Winemaking region of Catalonia, Spain.

co-op – Very many of France's good-quality, inexpensive wines are made by co-operatives. These are wine-producing centres whose members, and joint-owners, are local *vignerons* (vine growers). Each year they sell their harvests to the co-op for turning into branded wines. In Italy, co-op wines can be identified by the words *Cantina Sociale* on the label and in Germany by the term *Winzergenossenschaft*.

Corbières – A name to look out for. It's an AC of France's Midi (deep south) and produces countless robust reds and a few interesting whites, often at bargain prices.

Cortese – White grape variety of Piedmont, Italy. At its best, makes delicious, keenly brisk and fascinating wines, including those of the Gavi DOCG. Worth seeking out.

Costières de Nîmes – Until 1989, this AC of southern France was known as the Costières de Gard. It forms a buffer between the southern Rhône and Languedoc-Roussillon regions, and makes wines from broadly the same range of grape varieties. It's a name to look out for, the best red wines being notable for their concentration of colour and fruit, with the earthy-spiciness of the better Rhône wines and a likeable liquorice note. A few good white wines, too, and even a decent rosé or two.

Côte – In French, it simply means a side, or slope, of a hill. The implication in wine terms is that the grapes come from a vineyard ideally situated for maximum sunlight, good drainage and the unique soil conditions prevailing on the hill in question. It's fair enough to claim that vines grown on slopes might get more sunlight than those grown on the flat, but there is no guarantee whatsoever that any wine labelled 'Côtes du' this or that is made from grapes grown on a hillside anyway. Côtes du Rhône wines are a case in point. Many 'Côtes' wines come from entirely level vineyards and it is worth remembering that many of the vineyards of Bordeaux, producing most of the world's priciest wines, are little short of prairie-flat. The quality factor is determined much more significantly by the weather and the talents of the winemaker.

Coteaux Bourguignons – Generic AC of Burgundy, France, since 2011 for red and rosé wines from Pinot Noir and Gamay grapes, and white wines from (principally) Chardonnay and Bourgogne Aligoté grapes. The AC replaces the former appellation Bourgogne Grand Ordinaire.

Côtes de Blaye – Appellation Contrôlée zone of Bordeaux on the right bank of the River Gironde, opposite the more prestigious Médoc zone of the left bank. Best-rated vineyards qualify for the AC Premières Côtes de Blaye. A couple of centuries ago, Blaye (pronounced 'bligh') was the grander of the two, and even today makes some wines that compete well for quality, and at a fraction of the price of wines from its more fashionable rival across the water.

Côtes de Bourg – AC neighbouring Côtes de Blaye, making red wines of decent quality and value.

Côtes du Luberon – Appellation Contrôlée zone of Provence in south-east France. Wines, mostly red, are similar in style to Côtes du Rhône.

Côtes du Rhône – One of the biggest and best-known appellations of south-east France, covering an area roughly defined by the southern reaches of the valley of the River Rhône. The Côtes du Rhône AC achieves notably consistent quality at all points along the price scale. Lots of brilliant-value warm and spicy reds, principally from Grenache and Syrah grapes. There are also some white and rosé wines.

Côtes du Rhône Villages – Appellation within the larger Côtes du Rhône AC for wine of supposed superiority made in a number of zones associated with a long list of nominated individual villages.

Côtes du Roussillon – Huge appellation of south-west France known for strong, dark, peppery reds often offering very decent value.

Côtes du Roussillon Villages – Appellation for superior wines from a number of nominated locations within the larger Roussillon AC. Some of these village wines can be of exceptional quality and value.

crianza – Means 'nursery' in Spanish. On Rioja and Navarra wines, the designation signifies a wine that has been nursed through a maturing period of at least a year in oak casks and a further six months in bottle before being released for sale.

cru – A word that crops up with confusing regularity on French wine labels. It means 'the growing' or 'the making' of a wine and asserts that the wine concerned is from a specific vineyard. Under the Appellation Contrôlée rules, countless *crus* are classified in various hierarchical ranks. Hundreds of individual vineyards are described as *premier cru* or *grand cru* in the classic wine regions of Alsace, Bordeaux, Burgundy and Champagne. The common denominator is that the wine can be counted on to be expensive. On humbler wines, the use of the word *cru* tends to be mere decoration.

cru classé – *See* classed growth.

cuve – A vat for wine. French.

cuvée – French for the wine in a *cuve*, or vat. The word is much used on labels to imply that the wine is from just one vat, and thus of unique, unblended character. *Première cuvée* is supposedly the best wine from a given pressing because it comes from the free-run juice of grapes crushed by their own weight before pressing begins. Subsequent *cuvées* will have been from harsher pressings, grinding the grape pulp to extract the last drops of juice.

D

Dão – Major wine-producing region of northern Portugal now turning out much more interesting reds than it used to – worth looking out for anything made by mega-producer Sogrape.

demi sec – 'Half-dry' style of French (and some other) wines. Beware. It can mean anything from off-dry to cloyingly sweet.

DO – Denominación de Origen, Spain's wine-regulating scheme, similar to France's AC, but older – the first DO region was Rioja, from 1926. DO wines are Spain's best, accounting for a third of the nation's annual production.

DOC – Stands for Denominazione di Origine Controllata, Italy's equivalent of France's AC. The wines are made according to the stipulations of each of the system's 300-plus denominated zones of origin, along with a further 74 zones, which enjoy the superior classification of DOCG (DOC with *e Garantita* – guaranteed – appended).

DOCa – *Denominación de Origen Calificada* is Spain's highest regional wine classification; currently only Priorat and Rioja qualify.

DOP – Denominazione di Origine Protetta is an alternative classification to DOC (*qv*) under EU directive in Italy, comparable to AOP (*qv*) in France, but not yet widely adopted.

Durif – Rare black grape variety mostly of California, where it is also known as Petite Sirah, with some plantings in Australia.

E

earthy – A tricky word in the wine vocabulary. In this book, its use is meant to be complimentary. It indicates that the wine somehow suggests the soil the grapes were grown in, even (perhaps a shade too poetically) the landscape in which the vineyards lie. The amazing-value red wines of the torrid, volcanic southernmost regions of Italy are often described as earthy. This is an association with the pleasantly 'scorched' back-flavour in wines made from the ultra-ripe harvests of this near-sub-tropical part of the world.

edge – A wine with edge is one with evident (although not excessive) acidity.

élevé – 'Brought up' in French. Much used on wine labels where the wine has been matured (brought up) in oak barrels, *élevé en fûts de chêne*, to give it extra dimensions.

Entre Deux Mers – Meaning 'between two seas', it's a region lying between the Dordogne and Garonne rivers of Bordeaux, now mainly known for dry white wines from Sauvignon Blanc and Semillon grapes.

Estremadura – Wine-producing region occupying Portugal's coastal area north of Lisbon. Lots of interesting wines from indigenous grape varieties, often at bargain prices. If a label mentions Estremadura, it is a safe rule that there might be something good within.

Extremadura – Minor wine-producing region of western Spain abutting the frontier with Portugal's Alentejo region. Not to be confused with Estremadura of Portugal (above).

F

Falanghina – Revived ancient grape variety of southern Italy now making some superbly fresh and tangy white wines.

Faugères – AC of the Languedoc in south-west France. Source of many hearty, economic reds.

Feteasca – White grape variety widely grown in Romania. Name means 'maiden's grape' and the wine tends to be soft and slightly sweet.

Fiano – White grape variety of the Campania of southern Italy and Sicily, lately revived. It is said to have been cultivated by the ancient Romans for a wine called Apianum.

finish – The last flavour lingering in the mouth after wine has been swallowed.

fino – Pale and very dry style of sherry. You drink it thoroughly chilled – and you don't keep it any longer after opening than other dry white wines. Needs to be fresh to be at its best.

Fitou – AC of Languedoc, France. Red wines principally from Carignan, Grenache, Mourvèdre and Syrah grapes.

flabby – Fun word describing a wine that tastes dilute or watery, with insufficient acidity.

Frappato – Black grape variety of Sicily. Light red wines.

fruit – In tasting terms, the fruit is the greater part of the overall flavour of a wine. The wine is, after all, composed entirely of fruit

G

Gamay – The black grape that makes all red Beaujolais and some ordinary burgundy. It is a pretty safe rule to avoid Gamay wines from other regions.

Garganega – White grape variety of the Veneto region of north-east Italy. Best known as the principal ingredient of Soave, but occasionally included in varietal blends and mentioned as such on labels. Correctly pronounced 'gar-GAN-iga'.

Garnacha – Spanish black grape variety synonymous with Grenache of France. It is blended with Tempranillo to make the red wines of Rioja and Navarra, and is now quite widely cultivated elsewhere in Spain to make grippingly fruity varietals.

garrigue – Arid land of France's deep south giving its name to a style of red wine that notionally evokes the herby, heated, peppery flavours associated with such a landscape and its flora. A tricky metaphor.

Gavi – DOCG for dry aromatic white wine from Cortese grapes in Piedmont, north-west Italy. Trendy Gavi di Gavi wines tend to be enjoyably lush, but are rather expensive.

Gewürztraminer – One of the great grape varieties of Alsace, France. At their best, the wines are perfumed with lychees and are richly, spicily fruity, yet quite dry. Gewürztraminer from Alsace can be expensive, but the grape is also grown with some success in Germany, Italy, New Zealand and South America, at more approachable prices. Pronounced 'ge-VOORTS-traminner'.

Givry – AC for red and white wines in the Côte Chalonnaise sub-region of Burgundy. Source of some wonderfully natural-tasting reds that might be lighter than those of the more prestigious Côte d'Or to the north, but have great merits of their own. Relatively, the wines are often underpriced.

Glera – New official name for the Prosecco grape of northern Italy.

Godello – White grape variety of Galicia, Spain.

Graciano – Black grape variety of Spain that is one of the minor constituents of Rioja. Better known in its own right in Australia where it can make dense, spicy, long-lived red wines.

green – I don't often use this in the pejorative. Green, to me, is a likeable degree of freshness, especially in Sauvignon Blanc wines.

Grecanico – White grape variety of southern Italy, especially Sicily. Aromatic, grassy dry white wines.

Greco – White grape variety of southern Italy believed to be of ancient Greek origin. Big-flavoured dry white wines.

Grenache – The mainstay of the wines of the southern Rhône Valley in France. Grenache is usually the greater part of the mix in Côtes du Rhône reds and is widely planted right across the neighbouring Languedoc-Roussillon region. It's a big-cropping variety that thrives even in the hottest climates and is really a blending grape – most commonly with Syrah, the noble variety of the northern Rhône. Few French wines are labelled with its name, but the grape has caught on in Australia in a big way and it is now becoming a familiar varietal, known for strong, dark liquorous reds. Grenache is the French name for what is originally a Spanish variety, Garnacha.

Grillo – White grape of Sicily said to be among the island's oldest indigenous varieties, pre-dating the arrival of the Greeks in 600 BC. Much used for fortified Marsala, it has lately been revived for interesting, aromatic dry table wines.

grip – In wine-tasting terminology, the sensation in the mouth produced by a wine that has a healthy quantity of tannin in it. A wine with grip is a good wine. A wine with too much tannin, or which is still too young (the tannin hasn't 'softened' with age) is not described as having grip, but as mouth-puckering – or simply undrinkable.

Grolleau – Black grape variety of the Loire Valley principally cultivated for Rosé d'Anjou.

Gros Plant – White grape variety of the Pays Nantais in France's Loire estuary; synonymous with the Folle Blanche grape of south-west France.

Grüner Veltliner – The 'national' white-wine grape of Austria. In the past it made mostly soft, German-style everyday wines, but now is behind some excellent dry styles, too.

H

halbtrocken – 'Half-dry' in Germany's wine vocabulary. A reassurance that the wine is not a sugared Liebfraumilch-style confection.

hard – In red wine, a flavour denoting excess tannin, probably due to immaturity.

Haut-Médoc – Extensive AC of Bordeaux accounting for the greater part of the vineyard area to the north of the city of Bordeaux west of the Gironde river. The Haut-Médoc incorporates the prestigious commune-ACs of Listrac, Margaux, Moulis, Pauillac, St Estèphe and St Julien.

Hermitage – AC of northern Rhône Valley, France for red wines from Syrah grapes and some whites. Hermitage is also the regional name in South Africa for the Cinsaut grape.

hock – The wine of Germany's Rhine river valleys. Traditionally, but no longer consistently, it comes in brown bottles, as distinct from the wine of the Mosel river valleys – which comes in green ones.

Hunter Valley – Long-established (1820s) wine-producing region of New South Wales, Australia.

I

Indicación Geográfica Protegida (IGP) – Spain's country-wine quality designation covers 46 zones across the country. Wines made under the IGP can be labelled Vino de la Tierra.

Indication Géographique Protégée (IGP) – Introduced to France in 2010 under EU-wide wine-designation rules, IGP covers the wines previously known as vins de pays. Some wines are currently labelled IGP, but established vins de pays producers are redesignating slowly, if at all, and are not obliged to do so. Some will abbreviate, so, for example, Vin de Pays d'Oc shortens to Pays d'Oc.

Indicazione Geografica Tipica (IGT) – Italian wine-quality designation, broadly equivalent to France's IGP. The label has to state the geographical location of the vineyard and will often (but not always) state the principal grape varieties from which the wine is made.

isinglass – A gelatinous material used in fining (clarifying) wine. It is derived from fish bladders and consequently is eschewed by makers of 'vegetarian' or 'vegan' wines.

J

jammy – The 'sweetness' in dry red wines is supposed to evoke ripeness rather than sugariness. Sometimes, flavours include a sweetness reminiscent of jam. Usually a fault in the winemaking technique.

Jerez – Wine town of Andalucia, Spain, and home to sherry. The English word 'sherry' is a simple mispronunciation of Jerez.

joven – Young wine, Spanish. In regions such as Rioja, *vino joven* is a synonym for *sin crianza*, which means 'without ageing' in cask or bottle.

Jura – Wine region of eastern France incorporating four AOCs, Arbois, Château-Chalon, Côtes du Jura and L'Etoile. Known for still red, white and rosé wines and sparkling wines as well as exotic *vin de paille* and *vin jaune*.

Jurançon – Appellation for white wines from Courbu and Manseng grapes at Pau, south-west France.

K

Kabinett – Under Germany's bewildering wine-quality rules, this is a classification of a top-quality (QmP) wine. Expect a keen, dry, racy style. The name comes from the cabinet or cupboard in which winemakers traditionally kept their most treasured bottles.

Kekfrankos – Black grape variety of Hungary, particularly the Sopron region, which makes some of the country's more interesting red wines, characterised by colour and spiciness. Same variety as Austria's Blaufrankisch.

L

Ladoix – Unfashionable AC at northern edge of Côtes de Beaune makes some of Burgundy's true bargain reds. A name to look out for.

Lambrusco – The name is that of a black grape variety widely grown across northern Italy. True Lambrusco wine is red, dry and very slightly sparkling, and enjoying a current vogue in Britain.

Languedoc-Roussillon – Extensive wine region of southern France incorporating numerous ACs and IGP zones, notably the Pays d'Oc and Côtes de Roussillon.

lees – The detritus of the winemaking process that collects in the bottom of the vat or cask. Wines left for extended periods on the lees can acquire extra dimensions of flavour, in particular a 'leesy' creaminess.

legs – The liquid residue left clinging to the sides of the glass after wine has been swirled. The persistence of the legs is an indicator of the weight of alcohol. Also known as 'tears'.

lieu dit – This is starting to appear on French wine labels. It translates as an 'agreed place' and is an area of vineyard defined as of particular character or merit, but not classified under wine law. Usually, the *lieu dit*'s name is stated, with the implication that the wine in question has special merit.

liquorice – The pungent, slightly burnt flavours of this confection are detectable in some wines made from very ripe grapes, for example, the Malbec harvested in Argentina and several varieties grown in the very hot vineyards of southernmost Italy. A close synonym is 'tarry'. This characteristic is by no means a fault in red wine, unless very dominant, but it can make for a challenging flavour that might not appeal to all tastes.

liquorous – Wines of great weight and glyceriney texture (evidenced by the 'legs', or 'tears', which cling to the glass after the wine has been swirled) are always noteworthy. The connection with liquor is drawn in respect of the feel of the wine in the mouth, rather than with the higher alcoholic strength of spirits.

Lirac – Village and AC of southern Rhône Valley, France. A near-neighbour of the esteemed appellation of Châteauneuf du Pape, Lirac makes red wine of comparable depth and complexity, at competitive prices.

Lugana – DOC of Lombardy, Italy, known for a dry white wine that is often of real distinction – rich, almondy stuff from the ubiquitous Trebbiano grape.

M

Macabeo – One of the main grapes used for cava, the sparkling wine of Spain. It is the same grape as Viura.

Mâcon – Town and collective appellation of southern Burgundy, France. Minerally white wines from Chardonnay grapes and light reds from Pinot Noir and some Gamay. The better ones, and the ones exported, have the AC Mâcon-Villages and there are individual village wines with their own ACs including Mâcon-Clessé, Mâcon-Viré and Mâcon-Lugny.

Malbec – Black grape variety grown on a small scale in Bordeaux, and the mainstay of the wines of Cahors in France's Dordogne region under the name Cot. Now much better known for producing big butch reds in Argentina.

malolactic fermentation – In winemaking, a common natural bacterial action following alcoholic fermentation, converting malic (apple) acid into lactic (milk) acid. The effect is to reduce tartness and to boost creaminess in the wine. Adding lactic bacteria to wine to promote the process is widely practised.

manzanilla – Pale, very dry sherry of Sanlucar de Barrameda, a resort town on the Bay of Cadiz in Spain. Manzanilla is proud to be distinct from the pale, very dry fino sherry of the main producing town of Jerez de la Frontera an hour's drive inland. Drink it chilled and fresh – it goes downhill in an opened bottle after just a few days, even if kept (as it should be) in the fridge.

Margaret River – Vineyard region of Western Australia regarded as ideal for grape varieties including Cabernet Sauvignon. It has a relatively cool climate and a reputation for making sophisticated wines, both red and white.

Marlborough – Best-known vineyard region of New Zealand's South Island has a cool climate and a name for brisk but cerebral Sauvignon Blanc and Chardonnay wines.

Marsanne – White grape variety of the northern Rhône Valley and, increasingly, of the wider south of France. It's known for making well-coloured wines with heady aroma and nuanced fruit.

Mataro – Black grape variety of Australia. It's the same as the Mourvèdre of France and Monastrell of Spain.

Mazuelo – Spanish name for France's black grape variety Carignan.

McLaren Vale – Vineyard region south of Adelaide in south-east Australia. Known for blockbuster Shiraz (and Chardonnay) that can be of great balance and quality from winemakers who manage to keep the ripeness under control.

meaty – In wine-tasting, a weighty, rich red wine style.

Mencia – Black grape variety of Galicia and north-west Spain. Light red wines.

Mendoza – Wine region of Argentina. Lying to the east of the Andes mountains, just about opposite the best vineyards of Chile on the other side, Mendoza accounts for the bulk of Argentine wine production.

Merlot – One of the great black wine grapes of Bordeaux, and now grown all over the world. The name is said to derive from the French *merle*, a blackbird. Characteristics of Merlot-based wines attract descriptions such as 'plummy' and 'plump' with black-cherry aromas. The grapes are larger than most, and thus have less skin in proportion to their flesh. This means the resulting wines have less tannin than wines from smaller-berry varieties such as Cabernet Sauvignon, and are therefore, in the Bordeaux context at least, more suitable for drinking while still relatively young.

middle palate – In wine-tasting, the impression given by the wine after the first impact on 'entry' and before the 'finish' when the wine is swallowed.

Midi – Catch-all term for the deep south of France west of the Rhône Valley.

mineral – Irresistible term in wine-tasting. To me it evokes flavours such as the stone-pure freshness of some Loire dry whites, or the flinty quality of the more austere style of the Chardonnay grape, especially in Chablis. Mineral really just means something mined, as in dug out of the ground, like iron ore (as in 'steely' whites) or rock, as in, er, stone. Maybe there's something in it, but I am not entirely confident.

Minervois – AC for (mostly) red wines from vineyards around the Roman-founded town of Minerve in the Languedoc-Roussillon region of France. Often good value. The recently elevated Minervois La Livinière AC is a sort of Minervois *grand cru.*

Monastrell – Black grape variety of Spain, widely planted in Mediterranean regions for inexpensive wines notable for their high alcohol and toughness – though they can mature into excellent, soft reds. The variety is known in France as Mourvèdre and in Australia as Mataro.

Monbazillac – AC for sweet, dessert wines within the wider appellation of Bergerac in south-west France. Made from the same grape varieties (principally Sauvignon and Semillon) that go into the much costlier counterpart wines of Barsac and Sauternes near Bordeaux, these stickies from botrytis-affected, late-harvested grapes can be delicious and good value for money.

Montalcino – Hill town of Tuscany, Italy, and a DOCG for strong and very long-lived red wines from Brunello grapes. The wines are mostly very expensive. Rosso di Montalcino, a DOC for the humbler wines of the zone, is often a good buy.

Montepulciano – Black grape variety of Italy. Best known in Montepulciano d'Abruzzo, the juicy, purply-black and bramble-fruited red of the Abruzzi region midway down Italy's Adriatic side. Also the grape in the rightly popular hearty reds of Rosso Conero from around Ancona in the Marches. Not to be confused with the hill town of Montepulciano in Tuscany, famous for expensive Vino Nobile di Montepulciano wine, made from Sangiovese grapes.

morello – Lots of red wines have smells and flavours redolent of cherries. Morello cherries, among the darkest coloured and sweetest of all varieties and the preferred choice of cherry-brandy producers, have a distinct sweetness resembled by some wines made from Merlot grapes. A morello whiff or taste is generally very welcome.

Moscatel – Spanish Muscat.

Moscato – *See* Muscat.

moselle – The wine of Germany's Mosel river valleys, collectively known for winemaking purposes as the Mosel-Saar-Ruwer. The wine always comes in slim, green bottles, as distinct from the brown bottles traditionally, but no longer exclusively, employed for Rhine wines.

Mourvèdre – Widely planted black grape variety of southern France. It's an ingredient in many of the wines of Provence, the Rhône and Languedoc, including the ubiquitous Pays d'Oc. It's a hot-climate vine and the wine is usually blended with other varieties to give sweet aromas and 'backbone' to the mix. Known as Mataro in Australia and Monastrell in Spain.

Muscadet – One of France's most familiar everyday whites, made from a grape called the Melon or Melon de Bourgogne. It comes from vineyards at the estuarial end of the River Loire, and has a sea-breezy freshness about it. The better wines are reckoned to be those from the vineyards in the Sèvre et Maine region, and many are made *sur lie* – 'on the lees' – meaning that the wine is left in contact with the yeasty deposit of its fermentation until just before bottling, in an endeavour to add interest to what can sometimes be an acidic and fruitless style.

Muscat – Grape variety with origins in ancient Greece, and still grown widely among the Aegean islands for the production of sweet white wines. Muscats are the wines that taste more like grape juice than any other – but the high sugar levels ensure they are also among the most alcoholic of wines, too. Known as Moscato in Italy, the grape is much used for making sweet sparkling wines, as in Asti Spumante or Moscato d'Asti. There are several appellations in south-west France for inexpensive Muscats made rather like port, part-fermented before the addition of grape alcohol to halt the conversion of sugar into alcohol, creating a sweet and heady *vin doux naturel*. Dry Muscat wines, when well made, have a delicious sweet aroma but a refreshing, light touch with flavours reminiscent variously of orange blossom, wood smoke and grapefruit.

must – New-pressed grape juice prior to fermentation.

N

Navarra – DO wine-producing region of northern Spain adjacent to, and overshadowed by, Rioja. Navarra's wines can be startlingly akin to their neighbouring rivals, and sometimes rather better value for money.

négociant – In France, a dealer-producer who buys wines from growers and matures and/or blends them for bottling and sale under his or her own label. Purists can be a bit sniffy about these entrepreneurs, claiming that only the vine-grower with his or her own winemaking set-up can make truly authentic stuff, but the truth is that many of the best wines of France are *négociant*-produced – especially at the humbler end of the price scale. *Négociants* are often identified on wine labels as *négociant-éleveur* (literally 'dealer-bringer-up'), meaning that the wine has been matured, blended and bottled by the party in question.

Negroamaro – Black grape variety mainly of Puglia, the much-lauded wine region of south-east Italy. Dense, earthy red wines with ageing potential and plenty of alcohol. The name is probably (if not obviously) derived from Italian *negro* (black) and *amaro* (bitter). The grape behind Copertino, Salice Salentino and Squinzano.

Nerello Mascalese – Black grape of Sicily, most prolific in vineyards surrounding Mount Etna, making distinctive, flavoursome reds.

Nero d'Avola – Black grape variety of Sicily (Avola is a town in the province of Syracuse) and southern Italy. It makes deep-coloured wines that, given half a chance, can develop intensity and richness with age.

non-vintage – A wine is described as such when it has been blended from the harvests of more than one year. A non-vintage wine is not necessarily an inferior one, but under quality-control regulations around the world, still table wines most usually derive solely from one year's grape crop to qualify for appellation status. Champagnes and sparkling wines are mostly blended from several vintages, as are fortified wines such as port and sherry.

nose – In the vocabulary of the wine-taster, the nose is the scent of a wine. Sounds a bit dotty, but it makes a sensible enough alternative to the rather bald 'smell'. The use of the word 'perfume' implies that the wine smells particularly good. 'Aroma' is used specifically to describe a wine that smells as it should, as in 'this burgundy has the authentic strawberry-raspberry aroma of Pinot Noir'.

O

oak – Most of the world's costliest wines are matured in new or nearly new oak barrels, giving additional opulence of flavour. Of late, many cheaper wines have been getting the oak treatment, too, in older, cheaper casks, or simply by having sacks of oak chippings poured into their steel or fibreglass holding tanks. 'Oak aged' on a label is likely to indicate the latter treatments. But the overtly oaked wines of Australia have in some cases been so overdone that there is now a reactive trend whereby some producers proclaim their wines – particularly Chardonnays – as 'unoaked' on the label, thereby asserting that the flavours are more naturally achieved.

Oltrepo Pavese – Wine-producing zone of Piedmont, north-west Italy. The name means 'south of Pavia across the [river] Po' and the wines, both white and red, can be excellent quality and value for money.

organic wine – As in other sectors of the food industry, demand for organically made wine is – or appears to be – growing. As a rule, a wine qualifies as organic if it comes entirely from grapes grown in vineyards cultivated without the use of synthetic materials, and made in a winery where chemical treatments or additives are shunned with similar vigour. In fact, there are plenty of winemakers in the world using organic methods, but who disdain to label their bottles as such. Wines proclaiming their organic status used to carry the same sort of premium as their counterparts round the corner in the fruit, vegetable and meat aisles. But organic viticulture is now commonplace and there seems little price impact. There is no single worldwide (or even Europe-wide) standard for organic food or wine, so you pretty much have to take the producer's word for it.

P

Pasqua – One of the biggest and, it should be said, best wine producers of the Veneto region of north-west Italy.

Passerina – White grape variety of Marche, Italy. Used in blending but there is also a regional Passerina DOC.

Passetoutgrains – Designation for wine made from more than one grape variety grown in the same vineyard. French. Mostly red burgundy from Gamay and Pinot Noir.

Pays d'Oc – Shortened form under recent rule changes of French wine designation Vin de Pays d'Oc. All other similar regional designations can be similarly abbreviated.

Pecorino – White grape variety of mid-eastern Italy currently in vogue for well-coloured dry white varietal wines.

Periquita – Black grape variety of southern Portugal. Makes rather exotic spicy reds. Name means 'parrot'.

Perricone – Black grape variety of Sicily. Low-acid red wines.

PET – It's what they call plastic wine bottles – lighter to transport and allegedly as ecological as glass. Polyethylene terephthalate.

Petit Verdot – Black grape variety of Bordeaux contributing additional colour, density and spiciness to Cabernet Sauvignon-dominated blends. Mostly a minority player at home, but in Australia and California it is grown as the principal variety for some big hearty reds of real character.

petrol – When white wines from certain grapes, especially Riesling, are allowed to age in the bottle for longer than a year or two, they can take on a spirity aroma reminiscent of petrol or diesel. In grand mature German wines, this is considered a good thing.

Picpoul – Grape variety of southern France. Best known in Picpoul de Pinet, a dry white from near Sète on the Golfe de Lyon, lately elevated to AOP status. The name Picpoul (also Piquepoul) means 'stings the lips' – referring to the natural high acidity of the juice.

Piemonte – North-western province of Italy, which we call Piedmont, known for the spumante wines of the town of Asti, plus expensive Barbaresco and Barolo and better-value varietal red wines from Nebbiolo, Barbera and Dolcetto grapes.

Pinotage – South Africa's own black grape variety. Makes red wines ranging from light and juicy to dark, strong and long-lived. It's a cross between Pinot Noir and a grape the South Africans used to call Hermitage (thus the portmanteau name) but turns out to have been Cinsault.

Pinot Blanc – White grape variety principally of Alsace, France. Florally perfumed, exotically fruity dry white wines.

Pinot Grigio – White grape variety of northern Italy. Wines bearing its name are perplexingly fashionable. Good examples have an interesting smoky-pungent aroma and keen, slaking fruit. But most are dull. Originally French, it is at its best in the lushly exotic Pinot Gris wines of Alsace and is also successfully cultivated in Germany and New Zealand.

Pinot Noir – The great black grape of Burgundy, France. It makes all the region's fabulously expensive red wines. Notoriously difficult to grow in warmer climates, it is nevertheless cultivated by countless intrepid winemakers in the New World intent on reproducing the magic appeal of red burgundy. California and New Zealand have come closest. Some Chilean Pinot Noirs are inexpensive and worth trying.

Pouilly Fuissé – Village and AC of the Mâconnais region of southern Burgundy in France. Dry white wines from Chardonnay grapes. Wines are among the highest rated of the Mâconnais.

Pouilly Fumé – Village and AC of the Loire Valley in France. Dry white wines from Sauvignon Blanc grapes. Similar 'pebbly', 'grassy' or 'gooseberry' style to neighbouring AC Sancerre. The notion put about by some enthusiasts that Pouilly Fumé is 'smoky' is surely nothing more than word association with the name.

Primitivo – Black grape variety of southern Italy, especially the region of Puglia. Named from Latin *primus* for first, the grape is among the earliest-ripening of all varieties. The wines are typically dense and dark in colour with plenty of alcohol, and have an earthy, spicy style.

Priorat – Emerging wine region of Catalonia, Spain. Highly valued red wines from Garnacha and other varieties. Generic brands available in supermarkets are well worth trying out.

Prosecco – Softly sparkling wine of Italy's Veneto region. The best come from the DOCG Conegliano-Valdobbiadene, made as spumante ('foaming') wines in pressurised tanks, typically to 11 per cent alcohol and ranging from softly sweet to crisply dry. The constituent grape, previously also known as Prosecco, has been officially assigned the name Glera.

Puglia – The region occupying the 'heel' of southern Italy, making many good, inexpensive wines from indigenous grape varieties.

Q

QbA – German, standing for Qualitätswein bestimmter Anbaugebiete. It means 'quality wine from designated areas' and implies that the wine is made from grapes with a minimum level of ripeness, but it's by no means a guarantee of exciting quality. Only wines labelled QmP (see next entry) can be depended upon to be special.

QmP – Stands for Qualitätswein mit Prädikat. These are the serious wines of Germany, made without the addition of sugar to 'improve' them. To qualify for QmP status, the grapes must reach a level of ripeness as measured on a sweetness scale – all according to Germany's fiendishly complicated wine-quality regulations. Wines from grapes that reach the stated minimum level of sweetness qualify for the description of Kabinett. The next level up earns the rank of Spätlese, meaning 'late-picked'. Kabinett wines can be expected to be dry and brisk in style, and Spätlese wines a little bit riper and fuller. The next grade up, Auslese, meaning 'selected harvest', indicates a wine made from super-ripe grapes; it will be golden in colour and honeyed in flavour. A generation ago, these wines were as valued, and as expensive, as any of the world's grandest appellations. Beerenauslese and Trockenbeerenauslese are speciality wines made from individually picked late-harvest grapes.

Quincy – AC of Loire Valley, France, known for pebbly-dry white wines from Sauvignon grapes. The wines are forever compared to those of nearby and much better-known Sancerre – and Quincy often represents better value for money. Pronounced 'KAN-see'.

Quinta – Portuguese for farm or estate. It precedes the names of many of Portugal's best-known wines. It is pronounced 'KEEN-ta'.

R

racy – Evocative wine-tasting description for wine that thrills the tastebuds with a rush of exciting sensations. Good Rieslings often qualify.

raisiny – Wines from grapes that have been very ripe or overripe at harvest can take on a smell and flavour akin to the concentrated, heat-dried sweetness of raisins. As a minor element in the character of a wine, this can add to the appeal but as a dominant characteristic it is a fault.

rancio – Spanish term harking back to Roman times when wines were commonly stored in jars outside, exposed to the sun, so they oxidised and took on a burnt sort of flavour. Today, *rancio* describes a baked – and by no means unpleasant – flavour in fortified wines, particularly sherry and Madeira.

Reserva – In Portugal and Spain, this has genuine significance. The Portuguese use it for special wines with a higher alcohol level and longer ageing, although the precise periods vary between regions. In Spain, especially in the Navarra and Rioja regions, it means the wine must have had at least a year in oak and two in bottle before release.

reserve – On French (as *réserve*) or other wines, this implies special-quality, longer-aged wines, but has no official significance.

residual sugar – There is sugar in all wine, left over from the fermentation process. Some producers now mention the quantity of residual sugar on back labels in grams per litre of wine, even though so far there is no legal obligation to do so. Dry wines, red or white, typically have 3 g/l or fewer.

Above that, you might well be able to taste the sweetness. In southern hemisphere wines, made from grapes that have ripened under more-intense sunlight than their European counterparts, sugar levels can be correspondingly higher. Sweet wines such as Sauternes contain up to 150 g/l. Dry ('brut') sparkling wines made by the 'champagne' method typically have 10 g/l and tank-method fizzes such as prosecco up to 15 g/l.

Retsina – The universal white wine of Greece. It has been traditionally made in Attica, the region of Athens, for a very long time, and is said to owe its origins and name to the ancient custom of sealing amphorae (terracotta jars) of the wine with a gum made from pine resin. Some of the flavour of the resin inevitably transmitted itself into the wine, and ancient Greeks acquired a lasting taste for it.

Reuilly – AC of Loire Valley, France, for crisp dry whites from Sauvignon grapes. Pronounced 'RER-yee'.

Ribatejo – Emerging wine region of Portugal. Worth seeking out on labels of red wines in particular, because new winemakers are producing lively stuff from distinctive indigenous grapes such as Castelao and Trincadeira.

Ribera del Duero – Classic wine region of north-west Spain lying along the River Duero (which crosses the border to become Portugal's Douro, forming the valley where port comes from). It is home to an estate oddly named Vega Sicilia, where red wines of epic quality are made and sold at equally epic prices. Further down the scale, some very good reds are made, too.

Riesling – The noble grape variety of Germany. It is correctly pronounced 'REEZ-ling', not 'RICE-ling'. Once notorious as the grape behind all those boring 'medium' Liebfraumilches and Niersteiners, this grape has had a bad press. In fact, there has never been much, if any, Riesling in German plonk. But the country's best wines, the so-called Qualitätswein mit Prädikat grades, are made almost exclusively with Riesling. These wines range from crisply fresh and appley styles to extravagantly fruity, honeyed wines from late-harvested grapes. Excellent Riesling wines are also made in Alsace and now in Australasia.

Rioja – The principal fine-wine region of Spain, in the country's north east. The pricier wines are noted for their vanilla-pod richness from long ageing in oak casks. Tempranillo and Garnacha grapes make the reds, Viura the whites.

Ripasso – A particular style of Valpolicella wine. New wine is partially refermented in vats that have been used to make Recioto reds (wines made from semi-dried grapes), thus creating a bigger, smoother version of usually light and pale Valpolicella.

Riserva – In Italy, a wine made only in the best vintages, and allowed longer ageing in cask and bottle.

Rivaner – Alternative name for Germany's Müller-Thurgau grape.

Riverland – Vineyard region to the immediate north of the Barossa Valley of South Australia, extending east into New South Wales.

Roditis – White grape variety of Greece, known for fresh dry whites with decent acidity, often included in retsina.

rosso – Red wine, Italy.

Rosso Conero – DOC red wine made in the environs of Ancona in the Marches, Italy. Made from the Montepulciano grape, the wine can provide excellent value for money.

Ruby Cabernet – Black grape variety of California, created by crossing Cabernet Sauvignon and Carignan. Makes soft and squelchy red wine at home and in South Africa.

Rueda – DO of north-west Spain making first-class refreshing dry whites from the indigenous Verdejo grape, imported Sauvignon, and others. Exciting quality, and prices are keen.

Rully – AC of Chalonnais region of southern Burgundy, France. White wines from Chardonnay and red wines from Pinot Noir grapes. Both can be very good and substantially cheaper than their more northerly Burgundian neighbours. Pronounced 'ROO-yee'.

S

Sagrantino – Black grape variety native to Perugia, Italy. Dark, tannic wines best known in DOCG Sagrantino de Montefalco. Now also cultivated in Australia.

Saint Emilion – AC of Bordeaux, France. Centred on the romantic hill town of St Emilion, this famous sub-region makes some of the grandest red wines of France, but also some of the best-value ones. Less fashionable than the Médoc region on the opposite (west) bank of the River Gironde that bisects Bordeaux, St Emilion wines are made largely with the Merlot grape, and are relatively quick to mature. The top wines are classified *1er grand cru classé* and are madly expensive, but many more are classified respectively *grand cru classé* and *grand cru*, and these designations can be seen as a fairly trustworthy indicator of quality. There are several 'satellite' St Emilion ACs named after the villages at their centres, notably Lussac St Emilion, Montagne St Emilion and Puisseguin St Emilion. Some excellent wines are made by estates within these ACs, and at relatively affordable prices thanks to the comparatively humble status of their satellite designations.

Salento – Up-and-coming wine region of southern Italy. Many good bargain reds from local grapes including Nero d'Avola and Primitivo.

Sancerre – AC of the Loire Valley, France, renowned for flinty-fresh Sauvignon Blanc whites and rarer Pinot Noir reds and rosés.

Sangiovese – The local black grape of Tuscany, Italy, is the principal variety used for Chianti. Also planted further south in Italy and in the New World.

Generic Sangiovese di Toscana can make a consoling substitute for costly Chianti.

Saumur – Town and appellation of Loire Valley, France. Characterful minerally red wines from Cabernet Franc grapes, and some whites. Sparkling wines from Chenin Blanc grapes can be good value.

Saumur-Champigny – Separate appellation for red wines from Cabernet Franc grapes of Saumur in the Loire, sometimes very good and lively.

Sauvignon Blanc – French white grape variety now grown worldwide. New Zealand has raised worldwide production values challenging the long supremacy of French ACs in Bordeaux and the Loire Valley. Chile and South Africa aspire similarly. The wines are characterised by aromas of gooseberry, peapod, fresh-cut grass, even asparagus. Flavours are often described as 'grassy' or 'nettly'.

sec – Dry wine style. French.

secco – Dry wine style. Italian.

seco – Dry wine style. Spanish.

Semillon – White grape variety originally of Bordeaux, where it is blended with Sauvignon Blanc to make fresh dry whites and, when harvested very late in the season, the ambrosial sweet whites of Barsac, Sauternes and other appellations. Even in the driest wines, the grape can be recognised from its honeyed, sweet-pineapple, even banana-like aromas. Now widely planted in Australia and Latin America, and frequently blended with Chardonnay to make dry whites, some of them interesting.

sherry – The great aperitif wine of Spain, centred on the Andalusian city of Jerez (the name 'sherry' is an English mispronunciation). There is a lot of sherry-style wine in the world, but only the authentic wine from Jerez and the neighbouring producing centres of Puerta de Santa Maria and Sanlucar de Barrameda may label their wines as such. The Spanish drink real sherry – very dry and fresh, pale in colour and served well-chilled – called fino and manzanilla, and darker but naturally dry variations called amontillado, palo cortado and oloroso.

Shiraz – Australian name for the Syrah grape. The variety is the most widely planted of any in Australia, and makes red wines of wildly varying quality, characterised by dense colour, high alcohol, spicy fruit and generous, cushiony texture.

Somontano – Wine region of north-east Spain. Name means 'under the mountains' – in this case the Pyrenees – and the region has had DO status since 1984. Much innovative winemaking here, with New World styles emerging. Some very good buys. A region to watch.

souple – French wine-tasting term that translates into English as 'supple' or even 'docile' as in 'pliable', but I understand it in the vinous context to mean muscular but soft – a wine with tannin as well as soft fruit.

Spätlese – *See* QmP.

spirity – Some wines, mostly from the New World, are made from grapes so ripe at harvest that their high alcohol content can be detected through a mildly burning sensation on the tongue, similar to the effect of sipping a spirit. Young Port wines can be detectably spirity.

spritzy – Describes a wine with a gentle sparkle. Some young wines are intended to have this elusive fizziness; in others it is a fault.

spumante – Sparkling wine of Italy. Asti Spumante is the best known, from the town of Asti in the north-west Italian province of Piemonte. Many Prosecco wines are labelled as Spumante in style. The term describes wines that are fully sparkling. Frizzante wines have a less vigorous mousse.

stalky – A useful tasting term to describe red wines with flavours that make you think the stalks from the grape bunches must have been fermented along with the must (juice). Red Loire wines and youthful claret very often have this mild astringency. In moderation it's fine, but if it dominates it probably signifies the wine is at best immature and at worst badly made.

Stellenbosch – Town and region at the heart of South Africa's wine industry. It's an hour's drive from Cape Town and the source of much of the country's cheaper wine. Some serious-quality estate wines as well.

stony – Wine-tasting term for keenly dry white wines. It's meant to indicate a wine of purity and real quality, with just the right match of fruit and acidity.

structured – Good wines are not one-dimensional, they have layers of flavour and texture. A structured wine has phases of enjoyment: the 'attack', or first impression in the mouth; the middle palate as the wine is held in the mouth; and the lingering aftertaste.

sugar – *See* residual sugar.

sulphites – Nearly all wines, barring some esoteric 'natural' types of a kind not found in supermarkets are made with the aid of preparations containing sulphur to combat diseases in the vineyards and bacterial infections in the winery. It's difficult to make wine without sulphur. Even 'organic' wines need it. Because some people are sensitive to the traces of sulphur in some wines, worldwide health authorities insist wine labels bear the warning 'Contains sulphites'.

summer fruit – Wine-tasting term intended to convey a smell or taste of soft fruits such as strawberries and raspberries – without having to commit too specifically to which.

superiore – On labels of Italian wines, this is more than an idle boast. Under DOC(G) rules, wines must qualify for the *superiore* designation by reaching one or more specified quality levels, usually a higher alcohol content or an additional period of maturation. Frascati, for example, qualifies for DOC status at 11.5 per cent alcohol, but to be classified *superiore* must have 12 per cent alcohol.

sur lie – Literally, 'on the lees'. It's a term now widely used on the labels of Muscadet wines, signifying that after fermentation has died down, the new wine has been left in the tank over the winter on the lees – the detritus of yeasts and other interesting compounds left over from the turbid fermentation process. The idea is that additional interest is imparted into the flavour of the wine.

Syrah – The noble grape of the Rhône Valley, France. Makes very dark, dense wine characterised by peppery, tarry aromas. Now planted all over southern France and farther afield. In Australia it is known as Shiraz.

T

table wine – Wine that is unfortified and of an alcoholic strength, for UK tax purposes anyway, of no more than 15 per cent. I use the term to distinguish, for example, between the red table wines of the Douro Valley in Portugal and the region's better-known fortified wine, port.

Tafelwein – Table wine, German. The humblest quality designation, which doesn't usually bode very well.

tank method – Bulk-production process for sparkling wines. Base wine undergoes secondary fermentation in a large, sealed vat rather than in individual closed bottles. Also known as the Charmat method after the name of the inventor of the process. Prosecco is made by the tank method.

Tai – White grape variety of north-east Italy, a relative of Sauvignon Blanc. Also known in Italy as Tocai Friulano or, more correctly, Friulano.

Tannat – Black grape of south-west France, notably for wines of Madiran, and lately named as the variety most beneficial to health thanks to its outstanding antioxidant content.

tannin – Well known as the film-forming, teeth-coating component in tea, tannin is a natural compound that occurs in black grape skins and acts as a natural preservative in wine. Its noticeable presence in wine is regarded as a good thing. It gives young everyday reds their dryness, firmness of flavour and backbone. And it helps high-quality reds to retain their lively fruitiness for many years. A grand Bordeaux red when first made, for example, will have purply-sweet, rich fruit and mouth-puckering tannin, but after ten years or so this will have evolved into a delectably fruity, mature wine in which the formerly parching effects of the tannin have receded almost completely, leaving the shade of 'residual tannin' that marks out a great wine approaching maturity.

Tarrango – Black grape variety of Australia.

tarry – On the whole, winemakers don't like critics to say their wines evoke the redolence of road repairs, but I can't help using this term to describe the agreeable, sweet, 'burnt' flavour that is often found at the centre of the fruit in red wines from Argentina, Italy, Portugal and South Africa in particular.

TCA – Dreaded ailment in wine, usually blamed on faulty corks. It stands for 246 *trichloroanisol* and is characterised by a horrible musty smell and flavour in the affected wine. Thanks to technological advances made by cork manufacturers in Portugal – the leading cork nation – TCA is now in retreat.

tears – The colourless alcohol in the wine left clinging to the inside of the glass after the contents have been swirled. Persistent tears (also known as 'legs') indicate a wine of good concentration.

Tempranillo – The great black grape of Spain. Along with Garnacha (Grenache in France) it makes most red Rioja and Navarra wines and, under many pseudonyms, is an important or exclusive contributor to the wines of many other regions of Spain. It is also widely cultivated in South America.

Teroldego – Black grape variety of Trentino, northern Italy. Often known as Teroldego Rotaliano after the Rotaliano region where most of the vineyards lie. Deep-coloured, assertive, green-edged red wines.

terroir – French word for 'ground' or 'soil' has mystical meaning in vineyard country. Winemakers attribute the distinct characteristics of their products, not just to the soil conditions but to the lie of the land and the prevailing (micro)climate, all within the realm of terroir. The word now frequently appears on effusive back labels asserting the unique appeal of the wine. Some critics scoff that terroir is all imagined nonsense.

tinto – On Spanish labels indicates a deeply coloured red wine. Clarete denotes a paler colour. Also Portuguese.

Toro – Quality wine region east of Zamora, Spain.

Torrontes – White grape variety of Argentina. Makes soft, dry wines often with delicious grapey-spicy aroma, similar in style to the classic dry Muscat wines of Alsace, but at more accessible prices.

Touraine – Region encompassing a swathe of the Loire Valley, France. Non-AC wines may be labelled 'Sauvignon de Touraine'.

Touriga Nacional – The most valued black grape variety of the Douro Valley in Portugal, where port is made. The name Touriga now appears on an increasing number of table wines made as sidelines by the port producers. They can be very good, with the same spirity aroma and sleek flavours of port itself, minus the fortification.

Traminer – Grape variety, the same as Gewürztraminer.

Trebbiano – The workhorse white grape of Italy. A productive variety that is easy to cultivate, it seems to be included in just about every ordinary white wine of the entire nation – including Frascati, Orvieto and Soave. It is the same grape as France's Ugni Blanc. There are, however, distinct regional variations of the grape. Trebbiano di Lugana (also known as Turbiana) makes a distinctive white in the DOC of the name, sometimes very good, while Trebbiano di Toscana makes a major contribution to the distinctly less interesting dry whites of Chianti country.

Trincadeira Preta – Portuguese black grape variety native to the port-producing vineyards of the Douro Valley (where it goes under the name Tinta Amarella). In southern Portugal, it produces dark and sturdy table wines.

trocken – 'Dry' German wine. The description does have a particular meaning under German wine law, namely that there is only a low level of unfermented sugar lingering in the wine (9 grams per litre, if you need to know), and this can leave the wine tasting rather austere.

U

Ugni Blanc – The most widely cultivated white grape variety of France and the mainstay of many a cheap dry white wine. To date it has been better known as the provider of base wine for distilling into armagnac and cognac, but lately the name has been appearing on wine labels. Technology seems to be improving the performance of the grape. The curious name is pronounced 'OON-yee', and is the same variety as Italy's ubiquitous Trebbiano.

Utiel-Requena – Region and *Denominación de Origen* of Mediterranean Spain inland from Valencia. Principally red wines from Bobal, Garnacha and Tempranillo grapes grown at relatively high altitude, between 600 and 900 metres.

V

Vacqueyras – Village of the southern Rhône Valley of France in the region better known for its generic appellation, the Côtes du Rhône. Vacqueyras can date its winemaking history all the way back to 1414, but has only been producing under its own village AC since 1991. The wines, from Grenache and Syrah grapes, can be wonderfully silky and intense, spicy and long-lived.

Valdepeñas – An island of quality production amidst the ocean of mediocrity that is Spain's La Mancha region – where most of the grapes are grown for distilling into the head-banging brandies of Jerez. Valdepeñas reds are made from a grape they call the Cencibel – which turns out to be a very close relation of the Tempranillo grape that is the mainstay of the fine but expensive red wines of Rioja. Again, like Rioja, Valdepeñas wines are matured in oak casks to give them a vanilla-rich smoothness. Among bargain reds, Valdepeñas is a name to look out for.

Valpolicella – Red wine of Verona, Italy. Good examples have ripe, cherry fruit and a pleasingly dry finish. Unfortunately, there are many bad examples of Valpolicella. Shop with circumspection. Valpolicella Classico wines, from the best vineyards clustered around the town, are more reliable.

Those additionally labelled *superiore* have higher alcohol and some bottle age.

vanilla – Ageing wines in oak barrels (or, less picturesquely, adding oak chips to wine in huge concrete vats) imparts a range of characteristics including a smell of vanilla from the ethyl vanilline naturally given off by oak.

varietal – A varietal wine is one named after the grape variety (one or more) from which it is made. Nearly all everyday wines worldwide are now labelled in this way. It is salutary to contemplate that until the present wine boom began in the 1980s, wines described thus were virtually unknown outside Germany and one or two quirky regions of France and Italy.

vegan-friendly – My informal way of noting that a wine is claimed to have been made not only with animal-product-free finings (*see* vegetarian wine) but without any animal-related products whatsoever, such as livestock manure in the vineyards.

vegetal – A tasting note definitely open to interpretation. It suggests a smell or flavour reminiscent less of fruit (apple, pineapple, strawberry and the like) than of something leafy or even root based. Some wines are evocative (to some tastes) of beetroot, cabbage or even unlikelier vegetable flavours – and these characteristics may add materially to the attraction of the wine.

vegetarian wine – Wines labelled 'suitable for vegetarians' have been made without the assistance of animal products for 'fining' – clarifying – before bottling. Gelatine, egg whites, isinglass from fish bladders and casein from milk are among the items shunned, usually in favour of bentonite, an absorbent clay first found at Benton in the US state of Montana.

Verdejo – White grape of the Rueda region in north-west Spain. It can make superbly perfumed crisp dry whites of truly distinctive character and has helped make Rueda one of the best white-wine sources of Europe. No relation to Verdelho.

Verdelho – Portuguese grape variety once mainly used for a medium-dry style of Madeira, also called Verdelho, but now rare. The vine is now prospering in Australia, where it can make well-balanced dry whites with fleeting richness and lemon-lime acidity.

Verdicchio – White grape variety of Italy best known in the DOC zone of Castelli di Jesi in the Adriatic wine region of the Marches. Dry white wines once known for little more than their naff amphora-style bottles but now gaining a reputation for interesting, herbaceous flavours of recognisable character.

Vermentino – White grape variety principally of Italy, especially Sardinia. Makes florally scented soft dry whites.

Vieilles vignes – Old vines. Many French producers like to claim on their labels that the wine within is from vines of notable antiquity. While it's true that vines don't produce useful grapes for the first few years after planting, it is uncertain whether vines of much greater age – say 25 years plus – than others actually make better fruit. There are no regulations governing the use of the term, so it's not a reliable indicator anyway.

Vin de France – In effect, the new Vin de Table of France's morphing wine laws. The label may state the vintage (if all the wine in the blend does come from a single year's harvest) and the grape varieties that constitute the wine. It may not state the region of France from which the wine originates.

vin de liqueur – Sweet style of white wine mostly from the Pyrenean region of south-westernmost France, made by adding a little spirit to the new wine before it has fermented out, halting the fermentation and retaining sugar.

vin de pays – 'Country wine' of France. Introduced in 1968 and regularly revised ever since, it's the wine-quality designation between basic Vin de France and AOC/AOP. Although being superseded by the more recently introduced IGP (*qv*), there are more than 150 producing areas permitted to use the description vin de pays. Some vin de pays areas are huge: the Vin de Pays d'Oc (referencing the Languedoc region) covers much of the Midi and Provence. Plenty of wines bearing this humble designation are of astoundingly high quality and certainly compete with New World counterparts for interest and value. *See* Indication Géographique Protégée.

vin de table – Formerly official designation of generic French wine, now used only informally. *See* Vin de France.

vin doux naturel – Sweet, mildly fortified wine of southern France. A little spirit is added during the winemaking process, halting the fermentation by killing the yeast before it has consumed all the sugars – hence the pronounced sweetness of the wine.

vin gris – Rosé wine from Provence.

Vinho de mesa – 'Table wine' of Portugal.

Vino da tavola – The humblest official classification of Italian wine. Much ordinary plonk bears this designation, but the bizarre quirks of Italy's wine laws dictate that some of that country's finest wines are also classed as mere vino da tavola (table wine). If an expensive Italian wine is labelled as such, it doesn't mean it will be a disappointment.

Vino de la Tierra – Generic classification for regional wines, Spain. Abbreviates to VdT.

Vino de mesa – 'Table wine' of Spain. Usually very ordinary.

vintage – The grape harvest. The year displayed on bottle labels is the year of the harvest. Wines bearing no date have been blended from the harvests of two or more years.

Viognier – A white grape variety once exclusive to the northern Rhône Valley in France where it makes expensive Condrieu. Now, Viognier is grown more widely, in North and South America as well as elsewhere in France, and occasionally produces soft, marrowy whites that echo the grand style of Condrieu itself. The Viognier is now commonly blended with

Shiraz in red winemaking in Australia and South Africa. It does not dilute the colour and is confidently believed by highly experienced winemakers to enhance the quality. Steve Webber, in charge of winemaking at the revered De Bortoli estates in the Yarra Valley region of Victoria, Australia, puts between two and five per cent Viognier in with some of his Shiraz wines. 'I think it's the perfume,' he told me. 'It gives some femininity to the wine.'

Viura – White grape variety of Rioja, Spain. Also widely grown elsewhere in Spain under the name Macabeo. Wines have a blossomy aroma and are dry, but sometimes soft at the expense of acidity.

Vouvray – AC of the Loire Valley, France, known for still and sparkling dry white wines and sweet, still whites from late-harvested grapes. The wines, all from Chenin Blanc grapes, have a unique capacity for unctuous softness combined with lively freshness – an effect best portrayed in the demi-sec (slightly sweet) wines, which can be delicious and keenly priced.

Vranac – Black grape variety of the Balkans known for dense colour and tangy-bitter edge to the flavour. Best enjoyed in situ.

W

weight – In an ideal world the weight of a wine is determined by the ripeness of the grapes from which it has been made. In some cases the weight is determined merely by the quantity of sugar added during the production process. A good, genuine wine described as having weight is one in which there is plenty of alcohol and 'extract' – colour and flavour from the grapes. Wine enthusiasts judge weight by swirling the wine in the glass and then examining the 'legs' or 'tears' left clinging to the inside of the glass after the contents have subsided. Alcohol gives these runlets a dense, glycerine-like condition, and if they cling for a long time, the wine is deemed to have weight – a very good thing in all honestly made wines.

Winzergenossenschaft – One of the many very lengthy and peculiar words regularly found on labels of German wines. This means a winemaking co-operative. Many excellent German wines are made by these associations of growers.

woody – A subjective tasting note. A faintly rank odour or flavour suggesting the wine has spent too long in cask.

X

Xarel-lo – One of the main grape varieties for cava, the sparkling wine of Spain.

Xinomavro – Black grape variety of Greece. It retains its acidity even in the very hot conditions that prevail in many Greek vineyards, where harvests tend to over-ripen and make cooked-tasting wines. Modern winemaking techniques are capable of making well-balanced wines from Xinomavro.

Y

Yecla – Town and DO wine region of eastern Spain, close to Alicante, making interesting, strong-flavoured red and white wines, often at bargain prices.

yellow – White wines are not white at all, but various shades of yellow – or, more poetically, gold. Some white wines with opulent richness even have a flavour I cannot resist calling yellow – reminiscent of butter.

Z

Zibibbo – Sicilian white grape variety synonymous with north African variety Muscat of Alexandria. Scantily employed in sweet winemaking, and occasionally for drier styles.

Zierfandler – Esoteric white grape of Thermenregion, Austria. Aromatic dry wines and rare late-harvest sweet wines.

Zinfandel – Black grape variety of California. Makes brambly reds, some of which can age very gracefully, and 'blush' whites – actually pink, because a little of the skin colour is allowed to leach into the must. The vine is also planted in Australia and South America. The Primitivo of southern Italy is said to be a related variety, but makes a very different kind of wine.

Zweigelt – Black grape of Austria making juicy red wines for drinking young. Some wines are aged in oak to make interesting, heftier long-keepers.

Index

10-Year-Old Tawny Port, Finest 111
1531 Blanquette de Limoux Brut, Finest 112

A.A. Badenhorst The Curator White Blend 129
Agapi Kintonis Rosé 58
Alamos Malbec 88
Albariño, M&S Classics 75
Albariño Uruguay, Finest 111
Amandla Our Future Sauvignon Blanc 109
Amarone, Taste the Difference 90
Ambre Beaujolais Villages 79
Andrew Peace Chardonnay 43
Andrew Peace Shiraz 38
Animus Douro 25
Aprimondo Appassimento 101
Arc du Soleil Rosé 104
Arinto, M&S Found 74
Artesano de Argento Organic Malbec Fairtrade Rosé 42
Assyrtiko, The Best 83
Athlon Assyrtiko 28
Australian Cabernet Franc, Specially Selected 23
Australian Shiraz, Blueprint 116
Austrian Grüner Veltliner, Specially Selected 27
Austrian Riesling, Specially Selected 27
Azinhaga de Ouro Reserva 50

Babich Marlborough Sauvignon Blanc 109
Balfour Pinot Noir, M&S 65
Banfi Centine Toscana Rosso 120
Barbera d'Asti Superiore, M&S 67
Baron Amarillo Rioja Reserva 26
Baron Amarillo Rueda Verdejo 29
Barossa Chardonnay, Taste the Difference 91
Barossa Shiraz, Extra Special 32
Barossa Shiraz, Finest 98
Barossa Shiraz, M&S Classics No 37 64
Barossa Valley Shiraz, The Best 78
Beaujolais Cru Fleurie, Extra Special 33
Beaujolais Supérieur, Taste the Difference 88
Bersano Monteolivo Moscato d'Asti 132
Bethany 6 Gen Old Vine Grenache 39
Bonny Doon Le Cigare Orange 111
Bonny Doon Le Cigare Volant 104

Bordeaux Sauvignon Blanc, Taste the Difference 91
Bordeaux Supérieur 49
Boschendal Sommelier Selection Chardonnay 129
Bramble Hill Sparkling Brut 75
Buenas Vides Organic Argentinian Malbec, Specially Selected 23
Burra Brook Sauvignon Blanc 71
Burra Brook Shiraz, M&S 64

Cabernet Sauvignon, Co-op Fairtrade 38
Cahors Malbec, The Best 79
Cairanne Réserve des Hospitaliers 118
California Chardonnay, Taste the Difference 94
Californian Zinfandel, Co-op Irresistible 41
Cambala South African Sauvignon Blanc 29
Cambalala Fairhand Shiraz Pinotage 26
Cantina Segreti Castelão 122
Cape Kyala Chenin Blanc 109
Capeography Co Cape White Blend 84
Carignan, Co-op Irresistible 39
Carménère, Co-op Irresistible 39
Casa Maña Chardonnay 110
Casanova Corsican Rosé 42
Castel del Monte Rosso, Specially Selected 25
Castello Banfi Rosso di Montalcino 102
Castellone Organic Prosecco 30
Castellore Primitivo 25
Cava Brut, Asda 36
Cave de Turckheim Gewürztraminer 126
Cave des Roches Méditerranée Rosé 104
Cepa Allegro Rioja Reserva, Taste the Difference 90
Cepa Lebrel Rioja Blanco 51
Cepa Lebrel Rioja Joven 50
Cerceal, Waitrose Loved & Found 128
Chablis, Co-op Irresistible 44
Chablis, M&S Collection 72
Chablis, The Best 83
Champagne Brut, The Best 86
Champagne Charles Clément Brut 86
Champagne Delacourt Brut 76
Chapel Down Brut 130
Chapter & Verse Chardonnay 27
Chapter & Verse Merlot 23

Chardonnay, Extra Special 34
Château Barthès Bandol Rosé 42
Château Chapelle d'Aliénor 40
Château Recougne 55
Château Sénéjac 40
Château St-Hilaire Les Bouysses Cahors, Taste the Difference 89
Château St-Hilaire Médoc Cru Bourgeois Supérieur 119
Châteauneuf du Pape Clos Saint Michel 119
Châteauneuf du Pape, Finest 100
Chez Michel Bordeaux Merlot, M&S 66
Chez Michel Cahors, M&S 66
Chez Michel Fitou, M&S 65
Chez Michel Muscadet, M&S 72
Chianti Classico Riserva, Finest 101
Chianti Classico, The Best 80
Chianti Corte Alle Mura 49
Chilean Carmenere, The Best 78
Chilean Chardonnay, Specially Selected 27
Chilean Pinot Noir, The Best 78
Chinon, The Best 79
Cimarosa Merlot 49
Clocktower Pinot Noir, M&S 68
Cockburn's Fine White Port 111
Codorniu Vintage Organic Cava Brut 113
Collection St Emilion, M&S 66
ColleMassari Montecucco Rosso Riserva 121
Cono Sur Bicicleta Pinot Noir 32, 99
Cono Sur Bicicleta Viognier 34
Contevedo Cava Brut 30
Coonawarra Cabernet Sauvignon, Specially Selected 23
Corte Molino Prosecco 47
Costa Toscana Rosé, Specially Selected 26
Costières de Nîmes Réserve du Palais 117
Côte de Provence Rosé, Co-op Irresistible 42
Côté Mas Blanc 59
Coteaux de Béziers Merlot Syrah, Specially Selected 24
Coteaux de Béziers Rosé, Specially Selected 26
Coteaux de Béziers Viognier Grenache, Specially Selected 27
Côtes de Gascogne, Finest 106
Côtes de Provence Rosé, Definition 58
Côtes du Rhône Blanc, Taste the Difference 92
Côtes du Rhône, Co-op 39
Côtes du Rhône Pont de Fleur, M&S 65
Côtes du Rhône Pont de Fleur Rosé, M&S 70
Côtes du Rhône Villages Signargues, Finest 99

Crémant d'Alsace, Taste the Difference 94
Crémant de Bordeaux Rosé, Specially Selected 30
Crémant de Bourgogne Brut Blanc de Blancs 131
Crémant de Bourgogne, M&S Classics No 12 76
Crémant de Jura Brut, Specially Selected 29
Crémant de Loire Brut 52
Cune Cava Brut 62
Cune Mencia 81
CVNE Bodegas La Val Albariño 129
CVNE Rioja Gran Reserva, Taste the Difference 90

Dada Art 391 Malbec 88
Dão, The Best 81
d'Arenberg The Innocent Weed Organic Grenache Shiraz Mourvèdre 98
De Forville Nebbiolo 56
De Martino Organic Cabernet Sauvignon 117
Deluxe Barossa Valley Shiraz 49
Deluxe Fairtrade Chenin Blanc 51
Deluxe Limestone Coast Chardonnay 50
Demi-Sec Champagne, Sainsbury's 95
Des Tourelles Claret 99
Discovery Collection Bandol Rosé, Taste the Difference 91
Discovery Collection Luberon, Taste the Difference 92
Domaine des Ormes Saumur 39
Domini Veneti La Casetta Valpolicella Ripasso Superiore 56
Dr L Riesling 35
Dry German Riesling, Blueprint 127
Duffour Père et Fils Vinum Côtes de Gascogne 59

Ebenezer & Seppeltsfield Barossa Shiraz, M&S Collection 64
Eight Acres Sparkling Rosé, Co-op Irresistible 46
El Duque de Miralta Ribera del Duero, M&S 69
Elephant in the Room Voluminous Viognier 125
Emiliana Organic Malbec, M&S 65
Eminence de Bijou 124
English Sparkling Brut, Finest 112
English Sparkling Grand Reserve Brut, The Best 86
English White Cuvée, Specially Selected 27
Esprit des Trois Pierres Costières de Nîmes 117

Estevez Chilean Malbec 24
Estevez Chilean Merlot 24
Estevez Chilean Pinot Noir 24
Expressions Organic Negroamaro, M&S 68

Falanghina, Finest 108
Famille Perrin Côtes du Rhône Réserve 100
Famille Perrin Côtes du Rhône Réserve
    Blanc 107
The Federalist Chardonnay 129
Fête des Flaveurs Picpoul de Pinet 82
Feteasca Regala, M&S Expressions 74
Feteasca Regala, Wine Atlas 36
Finca Miguel Cava Brut 76
Finca Miguel Cava Brut Vintage 76
Fino Sherry, Finest 112
Fiori di Rosa 30
Fire Flower Shiraz 123
Floréal, Finest 106
Fonte del Re Lacrima di Morro d'Alba 102
Fronton Negrette Rosé, Taste the Difference
    91

G de Château Guiraud 45
Gavi di Gavi, The Best 83
Gelber Muskateller, Waitrose Loved &
    Found 125
Graham's 10-Year-Old Tawny Port 130
Gran Mascota Malbec 98
Gran Montana Uco Valley Malbec, The
    Best 78
Grapevine Chardonnay 29
Gratien & Meyer Crémant de Loire Brut
    112
Grüner Veltliner, Blueprint 125
The Guv'nor Sparkling NV 61

Hattingley Valley Classic Reserve 131
Heredad del Rey Monastrell Syrah 123
Hunawihr Alsace Pinot Gris 59

Il Grifone d'Oro Soave Classico 127
Ile de Beauté Rosé, Wine Atlas 33
Incanta Chardonnay 61
Incanta Pinot Noir 57
Interlude Pinot Noir 38
Isula Mea Syrah-Sciaccarellu Rosé 124

Joseph Drouhin Côte de Beaune 119
Journey's End Honeycomb Chardonnay 75
Jurançon Sec, Taste the Difference 92

Kakapo White 35
Kanonkop Kadette Pinotage 57
Ken Forrester The Misfits Cinsault 103

Kleine Kapelle Pinot Grigio 45
Kleine Zalze Reserve Shiraz 102
Klüsserather St Michael Riesling Feinherb
    51
Koha Pinot Grigio, M&S 74
Kooliburra Australian Shiraz Cabernet 23
Kopraas SMV, M&S 69

La Cascata Passivento, M&S 68
La Dame en Rose, M&S 69
La Ligne Rosé 104
La Maison du Vin Crémant de Loire 47
La Mora Maremma Toscana Rosso 33
La Perrière Touraine Sauvignon Blanc 125
La Petite Laurette du Midi Rosé 42
La P'tite Pierre Rouge 99
La Quaintrelle Côtes du Roussillon Villages
    Lesquerde 79
La Terrasse Chablis 93
La Vieille Ferme Rosé 34
Lateral Pinot Noir 99
Laurent Miquel Albarino Lagrasse 92
Laurent Miquel Vendanges Nocturnes
    Viognier 126
Le Bourgeron Chardonnay, Specially
    Selected 28
Le Froglet Shiraz, M&S 65
Le Mesnil Blanc de Blancs Grand Cru
    Champagne Brut 131
Le Sablou Sauvignon Blanc 125
L'Empreinte Rouge Lirac 118
Lentsch Zweigelt 116
Les Marennes Sancerre 119
Les Pionniers Champagne Brut 47
Les Terrasses Saint Nicolas de Bourgueil
    Cabernet Franc 100
Leyda Valley Pinot Noir, Extra Special 32
Lime Tree Australian Shiraz, Co-op 38
Lisboa, Taste the Difference 90
Lisboa Bonita, M&S 69
Lock Keeper's Reserve Chardonnay, M&S
    71
Luberon Blanc, Specially Selected 28
Lucido, M&S Found 73
Luna Dorada San Juan Shiraz, M&S 64
Lyme Bay Bacchus, M&S 71

M. Chapoutier Belleruche Côtes du Rhône 56
Mâcon-Villages, Co-op Irresistible 44
Maison du Vin Côtes du Gascogne 43
Maison Riveraine Morgon, M&S 66
Malbado Malbec 32
Malbec, Definition 55
Malbec, M&S Classics No 29 64
Manzoni Bianco, M&S Found 73

Mar de Frades Albariño Atlántico 110
Marcel Cabelier Crémant du Jura Brut 61
Marchesini Rosso 40
Margaux, Finest 100
Markus Molitor Sauvignon Blanc 51
Marlborough Sauvignon Blanc, Chosen by
    Majestic 60
Marlborough Sauvignon Blanc, Specially
    Selected 28
Marlborough Sauvignon Blanc, Taste the
    Difference 93
Marques de Almeida Albariño, Taste the
    Difference 94
Marques de Calatrava Reserva Tempranillo
    123
Marqués de los Rios Rioja Blanco Reserva,
    The Best 85
Marques de los Rios Rioja Reserva, The
    Best 82
Marques de los Rios Vintage Cava Brut, The
    Best 86
Marqués de Riscal Rioja Reserva 103
Marqués del Norte Rioja Reserva, Extra
    Special 33
Marzemino, M&S Found 67
Mathilde de Favray Pouilly-Fumé, M&S 72
Mimo Moutinho Dão 25
Minuty Rosé 124
Miraval Côtes de Provence Rosé 105
Montagne St Emilion, The Best 80
Montaudon Champagne Brut 52
Montepulciano d'Abruzzo, Finest 101
Montepulciano d'Abruzzo, M&S 67
Montepulciano d'Abruzzo, Taste the
    Difference 89
Moschofilero & Roditis, M&S Found 73
Mosel Steep Slopes Riesling, Finest 107
Mount Difficulty Pinot Noir 122
Mountain Vineyards Sauvignon Blanc 109
Muscadet Sèvre et Maine Sur Lie Château
    de la Petite Giraudière 44
Myrtia Moschofilero Assyrtiko Rosé, M&S
    70

Negroamaro, The Best 80
Nice Drop Shiraz 33
Nivola Lambrusco Grasparossa di
    Castelvetro 56
Norton Colección Malbec 116
Notte Stellata Primitivo di Manduria, M&S
    68

Old-Vine Garnacha, Co-op 41
Organic Aglianico Rosato, Loved & Found
    124
Organic Malbec, Co-op Fairtrade Irresistible
    38
Organic Susumaniello Rosato, Loved &
    Found 124
Orvieto Classico, Co-op 45

Paco Real Rioja Rosado, M&S 70
Palacio de Vivero Verdejo Rueda 36
Palladino Molise Biferno Riserva 40
Palo Cortado Sherry, The Best 85
Pasqua 11 Minutes Rosé 58
Passerina Terre di Chieti, Finest 108
Pata Negra Toro Roble 81
Paul Mas Marsanne Pays d'Oc 34
Paul Mas Picpoul de Pinet 44
Paul Mas Réserve Languedoc 118
Pazzia Primitivo di Manduria 121
Peacock Tail Pinotage, M&S 69
The Pebble Sauvignon Blanc 107
Pedro's Almacenista Selection Amontillado
    Medium Dry Sherry 130
Pet Nat Rosé Brut 75
Petit Chablis, The Best 82
Piccozza Pinot Bianco 128
Picpoul de Pinet, Chosen by Majestic 59
Picpoul de Pinet Le Rocher de Saint Victor
    51
Picpoul de Pinet, M&S Classics No 15 72
Picpoul de Pinet, Specially Selected 28
Pierre Jaurant Bordeaux 24
Pinot Grigio Trentino, Finest 108
Pinot Gris, Taste the Difference 94
Pinot Noir, Chosen by Majestic 55
Pinot Noir Vin de France 49
Poggio Baddiola 41
Pontenari Toscana Rosso, M&S 68
Pouilly-Fumé Domaine Masson-Blondelet
    126
Premier Cru Champagne Brut, Tesco Finest
    113
Primitivo, The Best 80
Primitivo Terre di Chieti, Finest 101
Primo Arte Primitivo, M&S 67

Régnié Cuvée Tim Domaine Pardon 118
Remy Ferbras Ventoux 117
Rheinhessen Pinot Noir, Taste the
    Difference 89
Ribera del Duero Ebela, Finest 103
Ribolla Gialla Spumante, Loved & Found
    131
Rioja Crianza, Chosen by Majestic 57
Rioja Reserva, Definition 57
Robert Oatley Signature Series Chardonnay
    43

Romanian Pinot Noir, Waitrose Blueprint 122
Rosé d'Anjou, M&S 70
Rosé Hola 105
Rully Montmorin Domaine Jean Chartron 45
Rustenberg Chardonnay 110

Saint Mont Grande Cuvée 106
Saint-Aubin 1er Cru Domaine Gérard Thomas 127
Santodeno Sicilia Grillo 83
Saperavi, M&S Found 67
Saumur Les Nivières 117
Sauvignon Blanc Semillon, Finest 105
Sedoso 41
Séptimo Sentido Verdejo 84
Shallow Bay Cabernet Sauvignon 102
Shaw + Smith M3 Chardonnay 58
Shiraz Rosé, Co-op Fairtrade 42
Sicilia Grillo, Taste the Difference 93
Soave, Morrisons 83
Soave Classico, Definition by Majestic 60
Soave Superiore Classico, Finest 108
Solo Pale Spanish Rosé, Co-op Irresistible 43
South African Sauvignon Blanc, The Best 84
South Point Pinot Grigio 61
St Hallett Faith Shiraz 98
Stellenbosch Chenin Blanc, Finest 109
Sturmwolken Riesling 93
Susumaniello Rosé, M&S Found 70

Tawny Port, Blueprint 129
Tbilvino Qvevris, M&S 72
Ten-Year-Old Tawny Port, The Best 85
Terre de Faiano Organic Nero di Troia 89
Terre di Faiano Organic Primitivo 120
Tewara Marlborough Sauvignon Blanc, M&S 74
Tierra y Hombre Pinot Noir, M&S 64
Tierra y Hombre Sauvignon Blanc 71
Tilimuqui Malbec 38
Tilimuqui Organic Fairtrade Malbec 116
Tilimuqui Sparkling Brut, Co-op Fairtrade 46
Toscana Rosso, Specially Selected 25
Touraine Sauvignon Blanc, Extra Special 35
Touraine Sauvignon Blanc, The Best 82
Touriga Nacional, Waitrose Loved & Found 122
Trapiche Vineyards Malbec 55
Tre Fiori Greco di Tufo 128
The Trilogy Malbec, Finest 98
Trimbach Pinot Blanc 60
Trimbach Riesling 35

Tyrrell's Brookdale Hunter Valley Semillon 106

Unearthed Bianco di Custoza 28
Unearthed Cigales Crianza 26
UVC Petit Chablis 107

Valdo Aquarius Rosé Brut 132
Valle de Leyda Chardonnay, Finest 106
Valpolicella Ripasso, Finest 101
Valpolicella Ripasso, The Best 81
Vanita Negroamaro 40
Vasavour Sauvignon Blanc 46
Ventoux, Taste the Difference 88
Ventoux Rouge, Specially Selected 24
Venturina Freisa d'Asti 120
Vermentino, M&S Expressions 73
Veuve Monsigny Champagne Brut 30
Veuve Olivier & Fils Secret de Cave Champagne Brut 36
Villa Cafaggio Chianti Classico 121
Villa Verde Montepulciano d'Abruzzo 80
Viña Albali Tempranillo Rosado 34
Viña Arana Rioja Gran Reserva 123
Viña del Cura Rioja Blanco, Finest 110
Viña del Cura Rioja Reserva, Finest 103
Viña Gala Rioja Blanco, Co-op Irresistible 46
Vinho Verde, Blueprint 128
Vinho Verde, M&S Classics 74
Vino Nobile di Montepulciano 50
Vintage Grand Cru Champagne Brut, Tesco Finest 113
Viòas del Rey Albariòo, Finest 110
Viognier, Co-op Irresistible 44
Viognier Paul Jaboulet Aîné 59
Von der Land Zweigelt 55
Von Kesselstatt Mosel Riesling 45

Waimea Estate Albariño 60
Welmoed Rosé 43
Western Australia Chardonnay, Finest 105
Western Australia Chardonnay, The Best 82
Wirra Wirra Church Block 32
Wolfberger Pinot Blanc 126

Yalumba Vigil Cabernet Shiraz 116
Ya'Po Sauvignon Blanc, M&S 71
Yealands Reserve Sauvignon Blanc 84
Yealands Sauvignon Blanc 35

Zacharias Assyrtiko 127
Zalze Shiraz Grenache Cabernet Franc Fairtrade 41